Rediscovering the Apostle Paul

Jesus Seminar Guides

Bernard Brandon Scott, series editor

Published volumes

Volume 1: Jesus Reconsidered: Scholarship in the Public Eye

Volume 2: Listening to the Parables of Jesus

Volume 3: Finding the Historical Jesus: Rules of Evidence

Volume 4: The Resurrection of Jesus: A Sourcebook

Volume 5: Rediscovering the Apostle Paul

Rediscovering the Apostle Paul

Bernard Brandon Scott, editor

POLEBRIDGE PRESS
Salem, Oregon

Cover and interior design by Robaire Ream

Library of Congress Cataloging-in-Publication Data
Rediscovering the apostle Paul / Bernard Brandon Scott, editor.
    p. cm. -- (Jesus seminar guides ; 5)
  Includes bibliographical references.
  ISBN 978-1-59815-028-5 (alk. paper)
  1. Paul, the Apostle, Saint. I. Scott, Bernard Brandon, 1941-
  BS2506.3.R43 2011
  225.9'2--dc22
                                                    2011006592

Table of Contents

Series Preface

Westar Institute, the home of the Jesus Seminar, is an advocate for literacy in religion and the Bible. A member-supported, non-profit research and educational institute, its mission is to foster collaborative research in religious studies and to communicate the results of the scholarship of religion to a broad, non-specialist public. Through publications, educational programs, and research projects like the Jesus Seminar, Westar brings Fellows of the Institute—scholars with advanced degrees in biblical studies, religion, or related fields—into conversation with non-specialists from all walks of life.

Westar's series, *Jesus Seminar Guides*, is designed to gather the best writings of Westar Fellows from the pages of its membership magazine, *The Fourth R*, its academic journal, *Forum*, and occasionally from previously unpublished material. Arranged topically, the *Guides* summarize the important questions and debates that have driven the work of the Jesus Seminar over the last twenty years. They are intended for use in classrooms, discussion groups inside and outside churches, and for the general reader.

Contributors

Gerd Lüdemann is Professor of History and Literature of Early Christian at Georg-August-University Göttingen, Germany. This "Obituary" is based on his book, *Paul: The Founder of Christianity* (Prometheus, 2002). Tom Hall, who worked with him on the book, revised the original version of this essay, which was translated from the German by Dr. John Bowden, and prepared this condensed version for *The Fourth R*. Lüdemann is a prolific author. Among his recent titles are *Eyes that See Not, The Pope Looks at Jesus* (Polebridge, 2008). After objections by the Protestant churches of Lower Saxony, Lüdemann was removed by the administration of the University from his chair in New Testament.

Heikki Räisänen was Professor of New Testament Exegesis at the University of Helsinki from 1975 to his retirement in 2006. His many books include *Paul and the Law* (1983), *Marcion, Muhammad and the Mahatma* (1997), and *Challenges to Biblical Interpretation* (2001).

Daryl D. Schmidt was Professor of Religion at Texas Christian University. A general editor of the Scholars Version translation project, he was the author of *The Gospel of Mark: Scholars Bible Edition* (1991) and editor of *Forum*, the scholarly magazine of Westar Institute. He was a member of the translation team for *The Authentic Letters of Paul* (2010).

James A. Veitch is Associate Professor in Security and Intelligence Studies at Massey University in Wellington, New Zealand. An ordained minister of the Presbyterian Church, he is the author of several books, including *Divergent Paths: Christians and Jews in the First Century* (1996) and *Christianity at the Crossroads* (1995). He previously served as Associate Professor of Religious Studies at Victoria University of Wellington.

John White is Emeritus Professor of Theology, Loyola
University of Chicago and a leading Paul scholar. Well-known
for his study of ancient Greek letters, he is author of *Light from
Ancient Letters* (1986). Recently, he produced a major study
The Apostle of God: Paul and the Promise of Abraham (1999).

Introduction

Bernard Brandon Scott

P aul has always been controversial. A number of his letters concern controversies. 1 and 2 Corinthians expose real conflict both with his own converts and with the so-called "super apostles" (2 Cor 11:5, 12:11). Galatians exposes a controversy with Cephas, the men from James, and even Barnabas (Gal 2:11–13).

Near the end of the first century the pseudonymous letter of James polemicizes against the Pauline notion of justification by faith. "You see that a person is justified by works and not by faith alone" (Jas 2:24). Ironically, it is from James that the "alone" so important for the Reformers comes into the debate. "Faith alone" does not occur in Paul's letters.

Somewhat later the pseudonymous author of 2 Peter actually refers to Paul by name, and thus indicates that his letters have already been collected and are being debated.

> So also our beloved brother Paul wrote to you according to the wisdom given him, speaking of this [patience] as he does in all his letters. There are some things in them hard to understand, which the ignorant and unstable twist to their own destruction, as they do the other scriptures.
> (2 Pet 3:15b–16)

In the history of interpretation Paul remains controversial. Just look at his role in the Protestant Reformation. In popular culture, Paul is often viewed antagonistically, charged with being against

1

women and the one who moved Christianity away from the pure
moral religion of Jesus. Even in modern scholarship the situation
of Paul remains an item of controversy, as the essays in this volume make clear.

Part of this problem goes back to the New Testament itself.
Sometimes I want to ask, "Will the real Paul please stand up!"
There are so many different Pauls in the New Testament that it
is hard to keep track of them, and as a result we tend to think of
Paul as—

- Contradictory
- Authoritarian
- Anti-female
- Arrogant
- Difficult to understand

Or you can draw up your own list.

Part of the problem with these different images is the fact that
Paul dominates the canon of the New Testament and so our view
of early Christianity. Simply count the pages of Nestle-Aland,
the standard scholarly Greek New Testament, and you will find
that over a third of those pages are ascribed to Paul. If you throw
in the Acts of the Apostles, half of which tells of his missionary
activity, then Paul appears on about half the pages of the New
Testament.

On the other hand, Peter, Jesus' follower, gets just fourteen
pages. Mary Magdalene, Jesus' devoted follower, is seldom mentioned—and even then is often viewed in such a derogatory
fashion that she eventually forfeits her reputation and becomes a
prostitute.

How, then, did Paul, who was not among Jesus' original followers, come to dominate early Christianity to the degree that
some have called him the inventor of Christianity?

Much of the difficulty in dealing with him is that much of
what is *said* to be from Paul is *not* from Paul.

A pivotal event in the development of early Christianity was
Rome's destruction of the Temple and the city of Jerusalem in
70 CE. In many ways early Christianity divides into events pre-
and post-70. When the destruction of the temple drove a wedge
between the followers of Moses and those of Jesus, synagogue

and church (*ekklēsia*) pulled apart and separated into two new and different religions.

Actually, pre-70 Christianity is not really Christian, but a second temple Jewish sect. The problem of terminology is really difficult but vitally important. How should pre-70 believers in Jesus as the Anointed be identified? Although most scholars struggle with this problem, no general agreement has been reached; and difficulties caused by this predicament run throughout these essays. Accordingly, we must confront this critical issue as we begin to come to terms with Paul. A reasonable way to begin is to say that pre-70 Christian groups operate within second temple Judaism and probably should not be called "Christian," whereas Post-70 Christianity defined itself over against Judaism and became a separate religion.

The canonical gospels and the Acts of the Apostles come from the period after 70, after the destruction of the temple, when Christianity was separating itself from Judaism, and Judaism was separating itself from Christianity. The canon itself comes from late second or third century, when complete separation had occurred.

Because Paul's authentic letters come from the period before 70, they are founded on different assumptions than those undergirding post-70 Christianity. And that raises the important question of which letters ascribed to Paul actually come from Paul? For the most part this is not a contentious issue among scholars. Strong agreement supports both the following list and the chronological order indicated:

- 1 Thessalonians
- Galatians
- 1 and 2 Corinthians
- Philippians
- Philemon
- Romans

These are taken to be the authentic Pauline letters for two primary reasons:

- They are situational. They deal with specific situations in particular communities.
- They deal with particular conflicts.

What these two reasons add up to is that these are real letters. They illustrate Paul interacting with real communities whose members are struggling to understand what it means to be followers of the Anointed.

It should also be noted that these letters come from a very narrow time span, having been written from the very late 40s through mid 50s. (See the *Authentic Letters of Paul* for a very good introduction to each letter and the problems of dating them.)

A second group consists of letters ascribed to Paul but of at best doubtful authenticity, since most scholars think they come not from Paul, but from the generation after him. These include

- 2 Thessalonians
- Colossians
- Ephesians

Colossians and Ephesians are the most prominent in this group. These letters differ from the authentic ones in that they do not address a specific situation in a particular community, but they deal with a theological idea. The difference is important, because Colossians and Ephesians deal primarily deal with a church—one that is understood in a much more hierarchical sense than we find in the authentic Pauline writings.

Yet another group of letters has now lost almost all acceptance among critical scholars as coming from Paul: these are the so-called Pastorals,

- 1 and 2 Timothy
- Titus

These letters do not address a church community, but individual disciples of Paul. They do not envision a particular community's problem, but are about controlling the church and passing on an existing tradition. Coming from the third or fourth generation after Paul, these writings reflect a church that now has bishops, elders, and deacons—an establishment of church officials not envisioned in the authentic letters. To be sure, "bishops and deacons" are mentioned in the greeting of the letter to the Philippians, but now we see a fixed order in the community: just as the Roman *pater familias* rules his family, the bishop rules his church. It is clear, for example, that contrary to the Apostle's proclamation of gender equality, women must be put in their place:

> [Younger widows] learn to be idle, gadding about from house to house; and they are not merely idle, but also gossips and busybodies, saying what they should not say. So I would have younger widows marry, bear children, and manage their households, so as to give the adversary no occasion to revile us. For some have already turned away to follow Satan. (1 Tim 5:13–15)

Colossians, Ephesians and the Pastorals present a hierarchical, female-controlling image of Paul, but the real Paul is quite different: "You are no longer Jew or Greek, no longer slave or freeborn, no longer male and female. Instead, you all have the same status in the service of God's Anointed, Jesus" (Gal 3:28 SV).

Still another image of Paul within the New Testament, one that has had a great influence on the way we perceive him, is the heroic Paul found in the last part of the Acts of the Apostles. Whether Paul would have recognized himself in that portrait is a major issue.

For example, the story of Paul's conversion derives from Acts and its dramatic imagery insures its dominance in the tradition. Paul, the persecutor of the young church on his way to Damascus with letters from the high priest, is struck off his horse, blinded by a heavenly flash of light. He hears a voice saying, "Saul, why are you persecuting me?" (Acts 9:4). Since the time of the Protestant Reformation, this scenario has informed both the major artistic representations of Paul and the way most Christians have perceived him.

Yet all of this comes from the author of Acts—except for the horse, which comes from artistic imagination. The oft-repeated details are missing from Paul's letters, where we find a much more circumspect and less dramatic description of the event. In Galatians he says:

> [W]hen the One who designated me before I was born and commissioned me to be an envoy, surprising all human expectations, chose to make his son known through me with the intent that I would proclaim God's world-transforming news to "the nations," I did not rush off to consult with anyone. (Gal. 1:15–16 SV)

Here, Paul clearly echoes the language of Isaiah and Jeremiah:

> Listen to me, O coastlands,
> pay attention, you peoples from far away!
> The LORD called me before I was born,
> while I was in my mother's womb he named me.
> (Isa 49:1)
>   …
> Before I formed you in the womb I knew you,
> and before you were born I consecrated you;
> I appointed you a prophet to the nations.
> (Jer 1:5)

Paul's use of prophetic diction and content indicates that he views what happened to him not as conversion, but as a special calling; like a prophet of Israel, he had been divinely commissioned to announce the gospel, "God's world-transforming news" (SV).

Paul does not convert, but Acts—written well after the destruction of the temple and maybe as late as the early second century (see Pervo, *Dating Acts*)—pictures him as *converting* from Judaism to Christianity and being instructed by Ananias.

Following up on Acts' clue, Augustine concluded that Paul was converted much as he, Augustine, had been converted when he repented of his former life and renounced paganism to embrace Christianity.

Paul did neither of these things. He thinks of himself as Jewish (Gal 2:15), and therefore he is not a pagan and already believes in the true God. Nor does he require moral conversion: "In regard to the requirements of the Law, I was flawless" (Phil 3:6 SV).

Luther, who made Augustine's conversion the paradigm for Protestant Christianity, thought he was following Paul; but he wasn't. He was following Augustine. The great modern interpreters of Paul in this matter are Rudolf Bultmann (1884–1976) and Karl Barth (1886–1968).

Fundamentally, our traditional interpretation of Paul has been determined first by Augustine and then Luther, and this interpretation has been a key ingredient in the development of modern theology. And unfortunately, as we have indicated, this does not yield Paul, but imposes the Christian conversion experiences of Augustine and Luther as the hermeneutical model for understanding Paul. Krister Stendahl, in his ground-breaking essay "Paul and the Introspective Conscience of the West," exposed this issue in 1963. We are still working out the implications. The essays in this volume appeared originally in *The Fourth R*, the magazine of the Jesus Seminar and its parent, the Westar Institute. These essays represent scholarly attempts to figure out what Paul is all about—and, as you will see, that a diversity of opinion, sometimes quite drastic, exists. As I have remarked, Paul is controversial. In his essay "Spotlight on Saint Paul," James Veitch has called for the Jesus Seminar to take up the Quest for the historical Paul—a grand idea, but one beset with problems. He noted that the Jesus Seminar voted on WHAT Jesus said or did, that is, whether or not a saying or deed went back to the historical Jesus. Thus the issue was, "what belongs to Jesus?" The Seminar did not directly address what the saying or happening *meant*. Even on the highly controversial issue of whether Jesus was an apocalyptic preacher, the group's conclusion was reached on the basis of the sorting of the data, not on what we thought Jesus meant by particular sayings or actions.

In Pauline studies the parallel problem is to decide what letters come from Paul, an issue that scholarship has for the most part settled (see the above discussion). There remain important questions concerning the editing of the letters, and they would provide important topics for the Seminar to take up (see *The Authentic Letters of Paul* and the essay by William Walker, "Pauline Interpolations" in *Problems in Understanding the Apostle Paul,* a companion volume to be published as Jesus Seminar Guide, vol. 6). But the real debate is not what Paul wrote, but what his letters mean, and how to understand them—and that debate is on display in the essays in this volume.

The opening essay by Gerd Lüdemann, "Paul—an Obituary," represents a traditional German Lutheran view of Paul. It falls within the line from Augustine to Luther to Bultmann. Lüdemann has a high degree of confidence in the accounts about Paul found in the Acts of the Apostles; he goes so far as to accept the historicity of Acts' account of Paul's speech at the Areopagus in Athens. For a scholar who is viewed in Germany as very radical, this is a highly traditional, even conservative understanding. But the radicalism lies elsewhere. Lüdemann thinks this

Paul is dangerous and has had a disastrous effect on the history of Christianity. In Lüdemann's judgment, Paul introduced into Christianity an intolerant, anti-Jewish leaning that became an anti-Semitic motif, and its ultimate tie to the Holocaust is hard to deny. Greek tolerance and rationalism, he argues, would have better served Christianity; and perhaps a reformed Judaism would have emerged as early Christianity and the subsequent history of the West would have been very different.

While Lüdemann's view of Paul is traditional, he recognizes that such an assessment is extremely dangerous, and by underlining its dark side he has led many scholars to question whether this traditional interpretation of Paul is correct.

The title of Heikki Räisänen's article, "A Controversial Jew: Paul and His Conflicting Convictions," lays bare his thesis. Like Lüdemann, he remains within the Lutheran tradition of interpretation of Paul, but argues that such a Paul is highly inconsistent. Both Räisänen and Lüdemann see in Romans 9–11 a primary source of conflict and contradiction. In both of their reconstructions, Paul is a Christian, even a founder of Christianity and therefore Judaism becomes the problem: in these key chapters, they argue, Paul is denying the validity of the Jewish Law, the Torah, while at the same time he employs seemingly contradictory arguments to rescue Israel without undermining his understanding of the new religion, Christianity. Lüdemann and Räisänen view Paul as highly inconsistent; they see him through Christian lenses and label him a Christian.

Both of these essays are important as the initial points of departure for this volume for two reasons:

- They provide a good summary of the traditional understanding of Paul against which the other essays in this volume are reacting in one way or another.
- They make evident the inconsistencies, contradictions and dangerous character of this traditional interpretation.

Lüdemann and Räisänen warn us that we either must abandon the old Paul or find a new Paul. But Räisänen in particular is critical of the effort to find a new Paul. He suspects that those who insist upon finding an inner consistency in Paul need Paul as an authority rather than a conversation partner.

James Veitch in "Spotlight on Saint Paul" sees F. C. Baur as pivotal in shifting the study of Paul from theology to history. Bauer accomplished this shift by locating Paul in an historical context, namely the debate between Jewish and Hellenistic Christianity. The reaction to Baur's effort to focus on the historical Paul parallels the reaction of the churches to the quest for the historical Jesus. Veitch isolates five questions emerging from Baur's work in the mid-nineteenth century that have dominated Pauline studies ever since and still remained unresolved. He traces the responses to these questions through the major figures in Pauline study. Seeing two dominant issues, apocalypticism and the Jewishness of Paul, he takes the reader on a tour of modern Pauline scholarship and its responses to these two leading questions. In my judgment, there is little debate about Paul's apocalypticism, but whether and how Paul is a Jew—or how Paul relates to Judaism and by implication Christianity—remains a major issue for debate.

In Veitch's essay we see an effort to take a broader focus so as to escape the paralyzing effect of traditional Pauline interpretation that Lüdemann and Räisänen have so clearly recognized. The way out for Veitch is a Paul seminar along the lines of the Jesus seminar, one that will tenaciously search for the historical Paul. While it poses a difficult task, his challenge is a valid one that still remains to be taken up.

White represents a genuine effort to articulate a new Paul by breaking out of the dogmatic traditions. He sees the challenge of Paul not in terms of Christology (Who is Jesus?), but of theology (Who is God?). For White, Paul is exploring a new, paradoxical view of God brought on by his experience of the resurrected Jesus. This experience forced Paul to conceive of God as the power by which life emerged out of sterility, and the result was that God became a creating parent.

Unlike Lüdemann and Räisänen, White does not see Paul as inconsistent, but entirely consistent, with his paradoxical view of God as the unifying factor. White also takes up Veitch's five problems from Baur and proposes a solution for each one.

Like White, Daryl Schmidt sought to find the unifying idea or consistency within in Paul. But unlike White who finds the consistency in Paul's paradoxical view of God, Schmidt approached the problem from the intellectual context of the Greco-Roman world, where the central issue is universalism or unity. He argues that in the notion of the oneness of God and accountability of all before God, Paul discovers the solution to the problem of universalism. He lays bare the steps in Paul's arguments as he develops them from the Septuagint, the Greek translation of the Hebrew Bible.

In following Schmidt's argument it is important to notice that at times his rendering of Pauline terms differs from the traditional English translation. This is particularly evident, for example in his translation the Greek word *pistis* as "trust" rather than the traditional "faith"—a variation that produces a somewhat different understanding. Schmidt was one of the translators of the new *Authentic Letters of Paul* (Polebridge, 2010), and one begins to see here the consequence of translation in our understanding of Paul.

In a second essay, "Paul: A New Perspective," White returns to the theme of the underlying consistency of Paul's thought. In his first essay White emphasized Paul's paradoxical view of God. In this essay his tack is slightly different. Stressing Paul's analogical thinking, he proposes that Paul is not concerned about the uniqueness of Jesus Christ or his death and resurrection, but how these concepts cohere analogically with other patterns. Here again, White is tracking down the metaphorical correlatives of what he argues is Paul's basic metaphor, God as parent.

Paul is, as was noted at the outset, radically controversial. The essays in this volume clearly indicate that. Lüdemann and Räisänen have shown the bankruptcy of the traditional understanding of Paul, while the other essays struggle to make sense of a "new" Paul. All of them show that we are still searching.

Chapter One

Paul—an Obituary

Gerd Lüdemann

Paul, from the great city of Tarsus in Cilicia, is rightly regarded as one of the most influential figures in the Christian West. At once a Jew, Roman, and a Christian, he saw himself above all as an apostle called by the risen Jesus to take the gospel to the Gentiles. But his life's work, dedicated to the service of the Risen Christ, only partly explains his tremendous importance.

The primary reason for this lasting impact is that Gentile Christians made Paul the pillar of their church and gave him a permanent place in it, first of all as the author of seven authentic letters which became part of the New Testament, and then as a writer to whom six further letters were attributed and accepted as scriptural. Not only do thirteen New Testament letters bear Paul's name as author, but Paul's example stimulated the collection of an additional seven "Catholic letters" incorrectly attributed to figures like Peter, James, and Jude, or indirectly ascribed to John.

Since the second part of Luke's Acts of the Apostles is devoted exclusively to Paul, he stands at the center of a third of the New Testament. It is no wonder that he had an overwhelming effect on church history. And in world history, Paul still played a deci-

The Fourth R 15,1 (2002), pp. 9–11, 18

sive role at the beginning of modernity. In the sixteenth century Western Christianity split over the interpretation of his doctrine of justification, a schism that still has incalculable consequences.

The Search for the Historical Paul

His significance for world history and the abundant Pauline literature make it eminently worthwhile to study him carefully. And the controversy over him will continue, because only now is the history of exegesis becoming an independent discipline and producing many new insights. Although welcome, such approaches make defining the historical Paul even more difficult. My thesis is that despite the two thousand years separating us from him, we can and should try to write a critical history of Paul in order to evaluate him in every respect. That is my aim in this obituary.

Paul was born around the same time as Jesus, some four hundred road miles north of his master's native Galilee. He was a Diaspora Jew who, having inherited Roman citizenship from his father, grew up in both the Jewish and Greco-Roman worlds. His basic education, mediated through Hellenistic Judaism, included instruction in the Greek language and rhetoric, and the macro-culture is reflected in his letters: Paul attended the theatre, followed contests in the arena, and witnessed philosophical feuds in the market place. In other words, he was imbued with both the breadth and beauty of the Hellenistic world, and its intrinsic rational temper.

But his ancestral religion also fostered a sense of belonging and a feeling of exclusiveness. Thoroughly steeped in Holy Scripture, he was no average Jew, but intensely devoted to the God who had chosen Israel and given it the commandments to live by. No wonder that he must study at the place where his heavenly Father had had the Temple built and where by divine grace daily sacrifice atoned for sin. Here at Judaism's epicenter the young zealot completed his education as a Pharisee, and here he wanted to work. His scholar's career, like that of his teacher Gamaliel, seemed predetermined.

But the Cilician synagogue he attended in Jerusalem included a group of Greek-speaking Jews devoted to a recently crucified holy man whom they hailed as Messiah and claimed to have been elevated by God. Equally unsettling were their neglect and even dismissal of the Law. As if a crucified Messiah was not bad enough! It was too much for Paul. As often with the elect of Israel, a zealous passion for the Law impelled him to attack this heterodoxy and nip it in the bud. Many fellow-countrymen, including his teacher Gamaliel, counseled patience and moderation, but the young zealot saw a dire challenge; and the subsequent development of this Diaspora group of Jesus-followers was to prove him right. The very suggestion that he was soon to play a key role in the dissemination of this deadly threat to Judaism would have taken his breath away.

A Radical About-face

Still, the inconceivable happened: in the midst of a bloody persecution, the very one whose followers he was pursuing appeared to Paul in heavenly guise, and suddenly Paul had no doubts. Surely this was the Son of God, and all that his followers said of him was true. Paul had no choice. He had to find a place in the community he had been persecuting. Since all this involved profound emotions, Paul temporarily lost his sight after the heavenly vision. But Ananais, his new brother in the faith, healed him in the name of Jesus and welcomed Paul into a faith which the erstwhile persecutor so far knew only in a rudimentary way.

As Paul reflected on Jesus' apparition and its significance, he recalled the scriptural passages prophesying a future Messiah; but how could he conceive of a Messiah who had suffered and died on a cross? Paul had never heard of a suffering Messiah. But since his encounter with the heavenly Lord utterly persuaded him that this was none other than the crucified Jesus, the ex-Pharisee's intimate knowledge of scripture provided a novel solution. In a bold leap of thought he combined the Jewish ideal of the Messiah with Isaiah's Suffering Servant—a leap made easier by the consideration that Jesus' suffering was only a transitional stage before his entrance into heavenly glory. And of course this would apply not only to Jesus; all Christians must suffer tribulation before the great Day.

Scripture also provided Paul a special role in the heavenly drama. Remembering that the prophets Isaiah and Jeremiah had claimed divine election, Paul applied this directly to himself (cf. Gal 1:15f.) and fantasized that like the two great prophets of the past he had been divinely ordained from his mother's womb to be a preacher. Hence the overweening self-confidence that exceeded even that of his pre-Christian period, and was the more extraordinary considering that this man from Tarsus never knew Jesus of Nazareth personally.

Could Paul derive his authority directly from the Lord without relying on those he had persecuted? What must he have experienced to justify his later claim to equal standing with the personal followers of Jesus? Indeed, Paul attributes the words of institution at the Lord's supper, which after all he must have learned in teaching from the community, to a direct communication from the Lord himself: "I received from the Lord what I also handed on to you. . . ." So also for other traditions about Jesus he learned: the authority of the Lord, who had personally commissioned Paul to be his apostle, automatically hallowed them. Believing himself in direct contact with the Lord, Paul received special indications as needed—he calls them revelations or mysteries—and immediately followed them.

But while heaven was almost always open, Satan might also castigate him if all those revelations went to his head. Still, he felt secure enough to invoke the power of Satan in such serious cases as that of the fornicator condemned in 1 Corinthians 5 so as to save both the community from uncleanness and the soul of the sinner from judgment. Furthermore Paul recognized that it was Satan who spread dissension in his communities in the form of false apostles. Yet whatever the adversity, Satan and his angels functioned only as predetermined by God, and had no power over Paul, his communities, or the rule of Him whose Son had come into the world to save people from sin.

As the agent of God and the Lord Jesus, Paul felt himself bound up in a cosmic drama of redemption whose pivotal issue was that salvation must include Gentiles, who need not first become Jews, but by faith in Jesus attained equal standing in the church of Christ. Such a view was repugnant to many Jewish Christians, but from the beginning Paul had experienced in an almost intoxicating way the unity of the church composed of Jews and Gentiles. He refers to this in two passages in which he quotes the baptismal liturgy: "There is neither Greek nor Jew, male nor female, slave nor free, but all are one in Jesus Christ" (Gal 3:26–28, cf. 1 Cor 12:13). This oft-repeated formula demolished all the barriers that the Torah had erected around Israel: "If anyone is in Christ there is a new creation; the old has passed away, behold, the new has come" (2 Cor 5:17). But this new cry of jubilation required the atoning death of the Son of God, as its continuation indicates: "All this (is) from God, who has reconciled us to himself through Christ"(2 Cor 5:18). And Paul continued to find new ways to proclaim the liberation: "If God is for us, who can be against us? For he did not spare even his only-begotten son, but has given him up for all of us . . ." (Rom 8:31–32).

The Seeds of Conflict

Paul's experiences of Christ in the present were Spirit-filled events which pointed to an even greater event, namely the consummation of the kingdom with the coming of Jesus on the clouds of heaven. Now Paul faced a problem. How was he to explain his visionary experiences to those in Jerusalem who had known Jesus personally and who similarly awaited the glory and the rewards of the coming kingdom? More important, how could he claim equal apostolic authority and an equally valid interpretation of the story of Jesus?

The history of Paul's relationship to the Jerusalem community shows that this was no easy task. A first visit, some three years after Paul's conversion, lasted two weeks and enabled him to make cautious contact with the leader of that community, Cephas, Jesus' first disciple. Besides Jesus' life and ministry, and the Easter experience, the Gentile mission was already an issue, and Paul was glad to arrive at agreements that would validate his apostleship in the greater Greek world. Then events came thick and fast. The mission to the Gentiles, which Cephas had agreed was Paul's task, proved extraordinarily successful, but Jewish-Christian communities also sprang up: Lydda, Joppa, Caesarea, Sidon, etc. Moreover, the "Holy Spirit", imagined as a mysterious and miraculous being, found acceptance and favor, first of all in Syria and then under the influence of Paul in Galatia, Macedonia,

and Achaea. A new movement was called to life by a man who
had never known Jesus personally, but was thus all the more in
contact with the heavenly Christ.

It was like a huge covered kettle full of water at a rolling boil:
to the energy generated by a growing number of Jewish disciples
was suddenly added an influx of Gentile converts, and the kettle
boiled over, the hissing and bubbling water creating new chan-
nels as it cooled, new communities composed of both Jews and
Gentiles. Naturally conflicts arose; strict Jewish Christians were
scandalized by non-observant activity in the mixed communities.
For Gentile Christians to repudiate the niceties of Torah practice
was one thing; for assimilation to endanger the identity of Jewish
Christians was quite another. The demand for strict segregation
of the Jewish Christians from their Greek brothers was inevitable:
in Paul's presence delegates from Jerusalem started a bitter dispute
over the purity of Jewish Christians in the mixed community of
Antioch. This put at risk all that had been achieved; and fourteen
years after his first visit to Jerusalem, it was revealed to Paul by his
heavenly Lord that he must return. Apparently he traveled with
an unbowed heart, for he took the uncircumcised Greek Titus
with him to establish a precedent. Not coincidentally, Paul's former missionary partner Barnabas was also a member of the party,
but so too were those strict Jewish Christians who, as Paul put it,
had crept into the community and provoked the dispute.

The situation in Jerusalem had changed. Cephas no longer
stood alone as leader, for Jesus' biological brother, James, now
stood at the head of a triumvirate consisting of himself, Cephas,
and John. It is illuminating that two personal disciples of Jesus
were junior to someone who, along with the rest of the family,
was skeptical about him during his lifetime.

After vigorous clashes in Jerusalem, an agreement was reached:
the Jerusalem church would spread the Good News among Jews,
Paul and Barnabas among Gentiles. More important than this
specific accommodation was the very fact of the accord; for it
provisionally rescued the unity of the church, and that was Paul's
main concern. Like so many treaties, this one allowed both parties to read their own understandings into it. Jews, for example,
included those in the Diaspora as well as those in the Palestinian
homeland. Further, the incendiary issue of people living in

mixed communities was not discussed at all. Worse yet, the agreement did not rule out a strict segregation of Jewish and Gentile Christians; in fact the agreement established a divisive condition. However, despite all the problems of the "formula of union" in Gal 2:9, there was agreement on the collection (Gal 2:10), which was to become an acid test for the relationship between the Gentile- and Jewish-Christian churches. Here there was no ambiguity. Paul and Barnabas would straightaway collect from his mission churches an offering to sustain the Jerusalem community. By giving Paul a lever to hold the Jerusalem people to their agreement, this also served as an instrument in church politics by confirming that his Gentile apostolate was the key element of a unified church. Without that unity, his mission to the Gentiles was null and void.

Paul had already envisaged a mission in Spain so as to conquer the last part of the world for his Lord; it was urgent for him to fulfill his destined role, for the Lord was near. But for now the agreement had to be safeguarded, and so Paul set out to secure the collection and cement the bond between his churches and Jerusalem. Accompanied by a staff of colleagues, Paul traveled through Galatia, giving detailed instructions for the collection, and sent his communities in Macedonia and Achaea instructions to do likewise. On the first day of every week the members were to set money aside in order to have a handsome sum ready for Paul to collect and deliver to the delegation that would take it to Jerusalem.

Of course, the journey served not only financial and political ends; Paul naturally initiated missions among new believers when, as in Ephesus, the occasion arose. Furthermore, the existing communities needed to be advised or exhorted in person or through delegates like Titus or Timothy.

Then disaster struck. Suddenly delegates from Jerusalem—the "false brethren" whom Paul had defeated there—now attacked him in his own communities and threatened to undo years of effort. They put his apostolic authority in question, introduced additional precepts of the law, and thus destroyed any fellowship between Paul and Jerusalem. The battle for the collection became the battle for the unity of the church. To assure the collection would be welcomed in Jerusalem, Paul decided to deliver it in person and again take up the battle he had won on two previous occasions.

The Fruits of Ambiguity

At the height of this conflict, shortly before he set off to Jerusalem, Paul wrote to the Roman church a letter no doubt intended for those in Jerusalem as well. In this memorable document the apostle proclaims his message of righteousness by faith, which is to be grasped in faith as free grace on the basis of the atoning death of Jesus and which is available to both Jews and Gentiles. Strangely, he does not seem to notice that in Romans 9–11 he partly takes back everything that he has written previously. Perhaps bewitched by an ethnocentricism he had ostensibly overcome, Paul promises that after "the fullness of the Gentiles be come in," all Israel will be saved—and he makes no mention of belief in Christ (Rom 11:26ff.). Being one of the chosen people suddenly appears more valuable than it did in the first eight chapters of Romans.

Paul indicates the reason for this about-face in the beginning of chapter 9: he grieves that the vast majority of his Jewish brothers have not accepted salvation in Christ, and would willingly suffer Christ's curse for their sake. Here we see another side of Paul. After the sharp attacks on the law in Galatians and in Romans 1–8, this may sound strange; but it attests to the ultimate priority of feeling over thought, in Paul as in nearly all humans.

A decade or two later, however, none of this was of any use to Jews. In the predominantly Gentile Christianity founded by Paul, the invention of a special Jewish salvation could not prevent unbelieving Israel from being damned to eternity, like the unbelieving Gentiles in a yet later period. The statement attributed to the risen Jesus in the secondary ending to Mark applies to both of them: "He who believes and is baptized will be saved, but he who does not believe will be condemned" (Mark 16:16; Editor's note: modern critical editions of the New Testament omit this "longer ending" of Mark's gospel as a later addition. See *The Complete Gospels*.)

Paul himself was to experience the Jewish Christian repudiation of the Gentile church. The collection he bore to Jerusalem was rejected, and hostile Christian brethren denounced him to the Roman authorities in order to get rid of him: he was charged with taking an Ephesian Gentile named Trophimus into the temple. The further course of events is well known. Fearing assassination by Jewish zealots, Paul appealed to the emperor and was safely taken to Rome, only to be executed there under Nero. He never made it to Spain.

However tragic these events, it is only fair to admit the factual basis of his opponents' charges. They claimed that Paul was teaching that Diaspora Jews should no longer circumcise their sons and was thus alienating them from Judaism. While this may be nowhere explicit in Paul's letters—he emphatically calls on Jews not to repudiate their circumcision—it must be conceded that the consequences of Paul's preaching largely validated the charge. In practice, the minority status of Jewish Christians in Pauline communities isolated them from their mother religion, and they ceased circumcising their male descendants. Sooner or later Jewish Christians lost their Jewishness in the Pauline communities. Furthermore, by proclaiming that grace is attained not by following the Law, but only through faith, the apostle's doctrine of justification led to ethical ambiguities (cf. Rom 3:8) and could easily be misconstrued as fostering libertinism.

Finally, Paul's theology of the Law was anything but clear. In fact, having abjured the Law, he made contradictory statements about Torah because he had already found his answer in the light of Christ. The Jewish side could no longer find common ground with such a man.

A further source of disaffection was that Paul had become a Gentile to the Gentiles, a Jew to the Jews, and thus in effect neither a Gentile nor a Jew. Where was his commitment? Throughout his public life he displayed not only a streak of arrogance but also a tendency to vacillation. It must have perplexed many, but as his accomplishments attest, this adaptability was a good way to succeed.

Defeat and Victory

Only when he attempted to lecture the intellectual elite of Athens did it run into a brick wall. The Stoic and Epicurean philosophers showed him his limits when he tried to impress them with future judgment through Christ and bodily resurrection. Despite his repeated (though sometimes deceptive) advocacy of reason, his religion, grounded in mystical experiences, was not up to the intellectual challenge of Greece. That he founded no community in Athens speaks volumes. One may also suspect that his remarks in 1 Corinthians about human wisdom being folly before God were at least partly an indirect rationalizing of the defeat in Athens.

Here it seems appropriate to note Paul's tenuous relationship to the Greek enlightenment. Paul did not arrive at truth through a mind trained to examine rigorously the content and viability of opposing views, to shun the phantasms of the imagination, and to acknowledge no authority over itself, whether divine or human. By contrast, the oriental mysticism we find in Hellenistic Christianity and its leading figure Paul has a supernatural character. It calls for uncritical surrender to authority and to divine guidance: the norm is not the intellect but the emotions, especially the mystical exaltation of the self seized by rapture. The spiritual man far outshines the logical man, for to him is disclosed the inscrutable truth which reason can never grasp.

But the fundamental reason for the victory of the Christianity of Paul and his pupils lay in the spirit of the time. The world had become weary of thought, and people found initiation into mysteries—of which baptism and the eucharist were but two of many—a less demanding way to confront their mortality. Ernest Renan's aphorism captures the ethos: The defeat of the human spirit while the public had become completely credulous.

Both the reaction against the Hellenistic Enlightenment and the orientalizing of the West paralleled an increasing authoritarianism in government, law, and social customs. The spirit of ancient Greece was throttled just as much as the constitutional ideal of the Roman state. Authority replaced research; faith preempted knowledge; the independent human spirit was made subservient to a cosmic deity; and slavish observance of divine commandments replaced the paradigm of responsible freedom. Hellenism marked the maturity of the ancient world; orientalism its downfall. This was the scene upon which Paul entered, and the drama in which he played a strong supporting role.

Triumphs and Tragedies

What did Paul's life yield? First of all, Christianity owes its existence to this Jew from Tarsus; he is its true founder. As he said, he worked harder than all the rest, for he laid the foundations for all future developments in the church. And by transplanting his misunderstanding of Jesus' religion to Gentile territory, he unintentionally formulated the lasting separation of the church and Israel. This in turn occasioned the tragic outcome of his work. The Christian anti-Judaism he inaugurated had a devastating effect. We may almost ask whether it would not have been better had Paul never lived. Might not Reformed Judaism with a Christian name have come into being, with the possibility of a humane faith which retained the priceless legacy of the mother religion? At any rate, without Paul and his disciples Judaism would never have been led into the abyss.

Besides, Paul's ideas often involve affronts to critical reason:

a. the notion that God's Son had to atone for the sins of the world;
b. the nonsensical identification of Jesus and the Christ, and with it the arrogant claim to be the spokesman of someone whom he never met;
c. the view that people should expect decisive help to result from mystical wishes;
d. his confused and arbitrary assertions about the Law;
e. the claim that an historical event provided for the eternal salvation of mankind

Even though we may understand a first-century enthusiast making such foolish claims, we have seen how dangerous they can prove when advocated by Christian churches and even by academic theologians. Some go so far as to propose an objective significance for Jesus' resurrection: that it is both the turning point of world history and an event of cosmic significance.

Paul was certainly the key figure in early Christianity, indeed its founder. But the view that his letters represent God's word is a crime against reason and humanity, and we should recognize that his way of thinking cannot guide our future, for lacking respect for "unbelievers" he summons them to obedience only to escape damnation. His monotheism is totalitarian, and his religious zeal too like the fanaticism which over two millennia has cost the lives of at least a million people per century.

One cannot deny Paul's human accomplishments nor doubt that they derived from his commitment to God. Unfortunately, conflict inevitably turns such a commitment against mere mortal men and women. *Soli Deo gloria.*

Chapter Two

A Controversial Jew

Paul and His Conflicting Convictions

Heikki Räisänen

Paul of Tarsus is a controversial figure. A quick Google search suggests that he is widely regarded as the real founder of Christianity. While this is hardly the majority view among specialists, it has had prominent representatives for more than a century now. Some interpreters maintain that Paul corrupted the message of Jesus along the way.

If Paul founded a new religion, this must imply that he left his ancestral religion, Judaism, and, indeed, this is what many scholars think. But these days a very different claim is also made: Paul remained a practicing "good Jew" who preached a "Law-respectful" gospel.

Perhaps there is a grain of truth in each picture. Paul himself says that he wishes to be "all things to all men" (1 Cor 9:22). He no doubt resorts to different rhetorical devices in different situations, but does this really account for all the different positions taken in his letters? Could it not be that there are conflicting tendencies in Paul's own mind? This is the track I am going to follow in this article, focusing on Paul's relation to his own Jewish roots.

The Fourth R 21,5 (2008), pp. 3–7, 24

I do not think that any single figure can be shown to be the founder of Christianity. The emergence of Christianity as a new religion, distinct from Judaism, was a long process, a chain reaction in which one thing led to another. Paul is clearly different from Jesus, and among New Testament authors he best embodies the reorientation that took place during the early decades. But Paul did not initiate the new development. Much of what distinguishes him from Jesus had been formulated by others before him, for instance the notion that Jesus' death had saving effects.

Paul's Jewish Past

Paul started his religious life as a Pharisee, as a member of a lay movement which took very seriously the belief that Israel was God's chosen people. Paul tells us that he "advanced in Judaism beyond many of his own age," being "extremely zealous" for the traditions of the fathers (Gal 1:14). This probably means that he devoted special attention to those customs which maintained a boundary between pure and impure, not least between Jews and non-Jews. If his tradition was in danger, he had to fight for it. In his later life he likewise fought for his new discoveries. The fact that the New Testament presents such a militant protagonist of the new faith as an exemplary figure has left a permanent imprint on Christianity, with the result that harsh polemics have often come to be regarded as a religious virtue.

Initially, Paul's zeal led him to oppose fanatically those who claimed that Jesus of Nazareth was God's Messiah. He had died on a Roman cross, but his followers claimed that God had raised him from the dead. For them this meant that the end-time of history had begun. Jesus was soon to return in glory to restore the kingdom of Israel and hold judgment over the living and the dead.

Paul and His Predecessors

There was nothing scandalous in such an expectation *per se*. Belief in a crucified Messiah might have seemed ridiculous, but what made it offensive was (it seems) the fact that some

Jesus people had ceased to observe the Torah, the Jewish law, in its totality. This was a group of "Hellenists"—Greek-speaking Diaspora Jews who had joined the Jesus movement—in Jerusalem gathered around one Stephen. Their story can be reconstructed only in very hypothetical terms from the Acts of Apostles (chaps. 6–8 and 11), but it seems that there was some tension between them and the "Hebrews" (the Aramaic-speaking Jesus-believers in Jerusalem), led by Peter. The relations between the Hellenists and non-Christian Jews worsened to the extent that Stephen was stoned to death in a riot. The author of Acts attributes his death to his liberal attitude toward the Torah and his criticism of the temple. The Stephen group may have allowed some Gentiles to join their Jewish community without the God-given entrance rite, circumcision, though we cannot be certain.

Stephen's friends had to flee Jerusalem. Acts reports that some of them landed in Antioch. There they addressed even Gentiles, and now (at the latest) the Jesus movement gained some uncircumcised male members. As so often, practice probably preceded theory. There are indications that ecstatic experiences played a part. Glossolalia (speaking in strange languages) was interpreted by some early Christians as proof that a person had received God's spirit. Some Gentiles started speaking in tongues before they had been formally converted. Such new experiences seem to have triggered a bold reinterpretation of Jewish tradition: God had shown that Gentiles could be accepted as members of his people without being circumcised. This meant that some requirements of the Torah could be side-stepped when fellowship with Gentile believers demanded it. Breaking social barriers became characteristic of the charismatic atmosphere of the movement. In a famous statement Paul quotes a slogan that might have originated in Antioch: "There is neither Jew nor Greek . . . for you are all one in Christ Jesus" (Gal 3:28). Despite all these developments, nothing indicates that the "Hellenists" consciously intended to separate from Judaism.

Be that as it may, Paul was one of those Jews who could not tolerate their actions, and he says himself that he had "persecuted" the followers of Jesus (Phil 3:6), whatever that means. At the very least he must have been engaged in violent polemics.

Perhaps he also tried to impose on them disciplinary measures such as flogging. In the course of this activity, however, a vision changed Paul's life. He saw what he took to be Jesus in heavenly glory. Whatever the nature of the experience, Paul inferred that the Jesus-believers were right, after all, in their claims about the Torah and the Gentiles. Paul claims that the vision made it clear to him that he had been called to work as a messenger to the Gentiles (Gal 1:15–16). This suggests that the mission to Gentiles had been the bone of contention between him and those he had "persecuted," and soon enough we find Paul in Antioch as a missionary of that community. In view of Paul's later ostentatious license with regard to the Torah, one can speculate that, in some sense, the Law may have been a (suppressed) problem for him all along—not as a demanding burden under which he was crushed, as an earlier generation of Protestant interpreters used to imagine, but as an entity that separated Jews from other peoples.

In Paul's time there were other Jews who were worried about the division of humankind. The Alexandrian intellectual Philo was perplexed by the apparent arbitrariness of the Torah (for example, its listing of some animals as unclean); he resorted to an allegorical interpretation of such laws. Others went further and gave up the practical observance of some precepts. Philo's critique of so-called "allegorists" shows where he draws the line— and also the fact that he himself is close to stepping over it. The real meaning, say, of the food laws is symbolic, but one should not therefore stop observing them. Philo's main point is, however, a social one: allegorists endanger their reputation in the community. Such reasoning suggests that, in opposing these allegorists, Philo combats a part of himself and reveals a tension inherent in his own life. But in the end Philo shows steadfast loyalty to his tradition, so much so that he can express heightened zeal against apostates.

To my mind Paul with all *his* tensions resembles a Philo who has given in to the enticements of the allegorists, following the lead of the Stephen circle. In some of his later statements on the Torah Paul does indeed put forward allegorical interpretations to the effect that Christians who do not follow the actual precepts of the Law nevertheless fulfill its true intention: "He is a Jew who is a Jew inwardly, and real circumcision is a matter of the heart, spiritual and not literal" (Rom 2:29); "Look out for those who mutilate the flesh. For we are the [true] circumcision, who worship God in spirit" (Phil 3:2–3).

In the course of his later debates with more conservative Jesus-believers, Paul went much further: he came to connect the Law with sin, curse, and death. The Torah, God's great gift in Jewish tradition, actually served the reign of Sin: its prohibitions incited people to transgress them, thereby involving them in sin and death (see especially Romans 7). While the Hellenists had shown some laxity with regard to the Law, they had not displayed anything like this kind of animosity, and the same is probably true of the early Paul as well.

Paul first became a missionary sponsored by the congregation of Antioch, the home-base of the Hellenists. But when his views grew more radical, the Antiochians broke with him, and he had to continue his work independently. He founded communities, preached a Law-free message about Jesus and encouraged Jewish and Gentile believers to live together without regard to purity regulations. He faced opposition not only from the synagogue but also from many Jesus-believers of Jewish birth. Most Jews regarded him as an apostate; and many Jesus-believers too suspected he was a heretic. Surely it would be a tremendous surprise for them if they could see what kind of status this man has gained as a Protestant saint! But Paul never ceased to regard himself as a Jew, and one of the relatively few true Jews at that.

A "Good Jew"?

Some scholars think that Paul was a practicing "good Jew" and that what he attacked was some false interpretation of the Law, not the Torah itself. It would be nice, of course, if he could be proved innocent of any denigration of the Jewish religion. But I think that Paul's relation to his Jewish heritage was ambiguous at best.

In order to maintain the view that Paul remained a good Jew one has to resort to tortuous interpretations of a number of passages (including 1 Corinthians 9, see below). This view leaves unexplained why Paul got the reputation of teaching Jews "to forsake Moses" and "not to circumcise their children"—that

such rumors had spread in Jerusalem is reported in Acts 21.
Conservative Jewish Christians in the second century still considered Paul their main enemy.

Paul picked and chose what he would and would not observe
from the Torah. He recommended through the model of his
own behavior that the food laws of the Torah could be relaxed
when table fellowship between Jewish and Gentile believers was
at stake. During his mission he had become largely indifferent to
important parts of the Torah. In a revealing passage Paul describes
his mission as follows: "To the Jews I became *as a Jew*, in order to
win Jews; to those under law I became as one under the law—
though *not being myself under the law*—that I might win those
under the law.... I have become *all things to all men*, that I might
by all means save some" (1 Cor 9:19–22).

Paul here discloses that, when he is among his kinsfolk, he acts
as if he were committed to the Torah, implying that deep down
he was not. Although he had by no means broken all continuity
with Jewish tradition, he had become internally alienated from
central parts of it. He felt free to choose. He could say to his
Gentile converts: "I have become as you are" (Gal 4:12). As the
Jewish scholar Daniel Boyarin notes, Paul's flexibility regarding
food laws "undermines any argument that Paul intended Jews to
remain Jewish, although Paul . . . would probably argue that he
was redefining Jewishness in such a way that everyone could be
Jewish" (*A Radical Jew*, p. 10).

Most scholars agree that Paul did not observe all of the Law
all of the time, but the significance of this is often not taken seriously. Many seem to think that circumcision and food laws are
minor issues anyway, so that Paul was plainly right in suggesting
that the whole Torah is fulfilled if only one observes the com-
mandment to "love your neighbor as yourself" (Gal 5:14). It is
even claimed that Paul's interpretation was a legitimate option for
Jews. But Paul would not have been judged on the basis of theological niceties. It would be a mistake to pay too much heed to
what he claims about himself. What counted was how other Jews
regarded his practice.

Paul mentions that he had to endure the synagogue punish-
ment of thirty-nine lashes no fewer than five times (2 Cor 11:24).
This shows that Paul kept returning to the synagogue and was

not considered an outsider: had he been one, he would not have been punished. On the other hand someone thus punished was certainly not regarded as a "good Jew." The vast majority of Paul's contemporaries considered his practice illegitimate.

Paul's Radical Stance in Galatians

Even Paul's theory is ambiguous. It began with the notion of equality: Gentiles need not subject themselves to circumcision in order to be part of God's people. Salvation is by faith (in Jesus as the Christ). But the conviction that Christ alone saves led to the satellite idea that even a Jew could not remain in a right relationship to God unless he or she embraced faith in Jesus as the Messiah. It should not be said (although it often is) that Paul merely extends Israel's covenant to embrace Gentiles as well. His very polemical letter to the Galatians makes it clear that no salvific covenant exists into which Gentiles could simply be included.

For Paul (Gal 3:6–14), the story of the forefather Abraham, who trusted God in a seemingly impossible situation, proves that "men of faith" (rather than those who cling to the Torah) are the true sons of Abraham, even if they be uncircumcised Gentiles. Paul redefines the descendants of Abraham as those who believe (in Jesus, that is). And he goes on to claim that the way of the faith excludes the way of the Law—and that observant Jews are under a curse. Christ has redeemed "us" (Jewish-born believers) from that curse and somehow this has opened for Gentiles the way to the God of Abraham. The Gentiles are never far from sight when Paul makes negative comments on the Torah. His famous language on the justification of sinners appears almost exclusively in contexts where he defends, in biblical language, the right of uncircumcised Gentiles to be members of his communities, without caring about "works of the Law."

Paul goes on to argue (Gal 3:15–18) that no additions can be made to a will; therefore the Law, here regarded as an addition to God's "will" to Abraham, is not valid. The Law was given to produce transgressions. Paul obliquely suggests (3:19–20) that the Torah may not even stem from God, but only from angels. He even compares observance of the Torah to pagan idolatry, asking: "How can you [former pagans who now consider circumcision] turn back again to the weak and beggarly elemental spirits, whose slaves you want to be once more?" (4:9–10) and even allows himself the joke of comparing circumcision to castration (5:12). The history of Israel as God's people is ignored. In effect, the church has replaced Israel as God's people.

Continuity or Discontinuity?

Paul's struggle in Romans 9–11

In Galatians, a letter written to a Gentile Christian community, the sacred heritage of the Jews is jeopardized. But when Paul is faced with Jewish-born Christians, we find him involved in a tortured struggle between two convictions. This is how I read the famous section Romans 9–11: Paul is struggling to make sense of a strong tension between his inherited values and his new convictions.

Paul exclaims in Rom 9:2–4:

> I have great sorrow and unceasing anguish in my heart. For I could wish that I myself were accursed and cut off from Christ for the sake of my brethren, my kinsmen by race. They are Israelites, and to them belong the sonship, the glory, the covenants, the giving of the law, the worship and the promises; to them belong the patriarchs, and of their race, according to the flesh, is the Christ.

Yet what will Israelites gain from all these advantages (which must come as a surprise to a reader of Galatians), if they remain outside the salvation in Christ?

God's integrity is at stake: has his word failed? Paul answers by redefining "Israel" (Rom 9:6–13): all those who are "of Israel" (the ethnic people) do not really belong to Israel. Who belongs and who does not is freely decreed by God. God is wholly sovereign in his decisions: he has always called some, like Jacob, and not others, like Esau "even before they had been born or had done anything good or bad." It follows that the gospel is not being rejected by the elect of God, for the majority of ethnic Israel never belonged to the elect. The gospel is being rejected by the non-elect and accepted by the true "Israel." Everything is as God meant it to be. The price for this relief is the implication

(not stated in so many words) that there never was a covenant for
Israel as an ethnic people. At this point the argument fully agrees
with that of Galatians.

Paul goes to great lengths to undergird the thesis of God's free
election (Rom 9:14–18): not only does God freely choose whom
he wants to be saved; he just as freely "hardens the heart of
whomever he wills." The more perceptive commentators deplore
Paul portrayal of God as a tyrant. Even Paul himself senses that a
moral problem is involved: how can humans be held responsible
if everything is effected by God? But all he can do is to assert
that the Great Potter has the right to create what he wants, even
"vessels of wrath" prepared for destruction (9:22). The unbelieving Jews of Paul's time are such vessels. Paul tries to use Scripture
to show that God always intended to call Gentiles to be his sons
as well; of Israel only a remnant will be saved (9:24–29). Romans
9:6–29 gives a clear answer to the question, Has God's word
failed? No, for God never promised anything for ethnic Israel.

Undoubtedly Paul always has Jewish *Christians* in mind when
he speaks of God's merciful election. The shape of Paul's argument prevents him, however, from spelling this out. He cannot
state at this point that faith in Jesus is a condition of belonging
to God's people. Any mention of faith, generally so important to
Paul, would damage his present argument, for here he speaks as if
humans are saved simply by God's arbitrary action: their destinies
are decreed before they are born. This sounds like a rigid doctrine of double predestination (the belief that God decides before
birth who will and who will not be saved). But Paul is not devel-
oping a doctrine. He is wrestling with the burning practical issue
that Israel does not accept his message. Double predestination
emerges as a side effect, as a tentative solution which Paul tries
and then quietly drops. Future generations of Christians would
have been spared a great deal of anxiety and despair, if Paul had
not tried it at all.

The idea of predestination is dropped in the very next section (Rom 9:30–10:21). There Paul explains why Israel, now seen
as an ethnic entity after all, has failed to attain righteousness—a
right relationship to God—whereas (some) Gentiles have found
it. We now hear nothing about the divine election of some and
the "hardening" of others. On the contrary, God held out his

hands toward Israel "all day long," patiently inviting her to salvation, but Israel remained "a disobedient and contrary people." She refused to obey God and to accept his action in Christ with faith. Salvation is meant for everyone who believes (in Christ); "everyone who calls on the name of the Lord (Christ) will be saved."

Then, however, Paul suddenly asserts that God can*not* have rejected his people, ethnic Israel, after all (11:1–2). This is surprising given chapter 9, but it continues the argument about the remnant. Ethnic Israel has split in two—the chosen remnant and the hardened majority. Paul goes on to suggest that the hardening of Israel has a positive purpose: it somehow serves to bring salvation to the Gentiles. In 11:17–24 he presents a parable of an olive tree (Israel) from which some branches have been broken off and onto which branches of a wild tree have been grafted. In effect he is claiming that, on the whole, Israel remains God's people; some apostates have been excluded and some believing Gentiles have been included. The situation is caused by the unbelief of "some," by human failure, not by a divine decree. Gentiles are admonished to remain faithful so that they will not be "broken off" as well. Here the idea of divine hardening, so vigorously set forth shortly before, would be out of place: what matters is human perseverance in faith. But God has the power to graft back again those Israelites who have fallen, "if they do not persist in their unbelief."

And indeed a miracle will happen. Paul's discloses a mystery: the hardening will not be final. Apparently in connection with Jesus' return, when the "full number of the Gentiles" has "come in," *all Israel*—the whole people, not just a remnant—will be saved (11:25). This will happen because the Israelites are "beloved for the sake of their ancestors;" "the gifts and the call of God are irrevocable" (11:29).

The bold idea of the salvation of all Israel differs completely from Paul's attitude to Israel in Galatians. Therefore some scholars assume that Paul's theology underwent a substantial development between Galatians and Romans. But the thesis presented at the end of Romans 11 is also quite different from the thesis argued a couple of pages earlier in chapter 9. This fact works against the development theory (unless one assumes that Paul's theology took quite a new turn during a hypothetical dictation break between, say, Romans 10 and Romans 11).

Recently a novel interpretation of Romans 11 has gained some ground: Paul presupposes that Israel will be saved independently of Christ's work, simply on the basis of God's covenant with Abraham. Paul is thought to maintain a theology of two covenants: Jews will be saved because of the covenant with the patriarchs and Gentile Christians because of the new covenant established in Christ. The idea is admirable in its ecumenical scope, but there is little evidence for it. Romans 11 is a tenuous basis for an assertion which would nullify everything that Paul writes elsewhere (including Romans 10) about the crucial significance of Jesus for all humanity, first for the Jews (!) and also for the Greeks. The idea of the salvation of all Israel is at odds with Paul's other statements and has rightly been called a desperate theory. When Paul ends up by emphasizing that God's promises to Israel will remain valid after all, he is in fact defending his own mission: what happens in the near future will justify his liberal practice that had upset born Jews. From the viewpoint of a non-Christian Jew, Paul's statement of the salvation of all Israel is not so generous as many Christians tend to think. In effect Paul is saying that the Jews will be saved, since they will become like us.

Paul's arguments fluctuate back and forth, as if he is desperately trying to solve a problem which proves to be too difficult. He tries different solutions:

1. Israel as a people was never chosen. God has elected in advance only a small "remnant" to be saved. The others he has prepared from the beginning for destruction; they have been hardened by him. Salvation depends on God's arbitrary choice.

2. God has not hardened anyone. Israel herself has been stubborn. Those (Jews or Gentiles) who accept Christ in faith will be saved.

3. God has provisionally hardened the great majority of Israel. In the end, however, the whole people will be saved, since God had once elected it. Salvation is based on the promises given to the patriarchs of Israel.

Compared with the general tenor of Paul's letters, the first
solution goes "too far," as the argument leaves no room for faith.
The idea of double predestination appears as an argument which
Paul tries, but soon drops. The third solution goes too far in the
opposite direction; the logic of that argument would lead to the
notion of universal restoration of all: "God has imprisoned *all* in
disobedience so that he may be merciful to *all*" (Rom 11:32).
Here, too, faith seems optional; God's overwhelming grace is
enough. The most "normal" passage in the section is the middle
one which stresses the significance of a faith decision (Rom
9:30–10:21, especially 10:4–13).

With all its tensions, Romans 9–11 illustrates how central and
how difficult questions of identity and continuity were for Paul.
It shows him in a struggle to legitimate his mission and to assert
his little group's identity in terms of traditional values. If God has
made Jesus Christ the only road to salvation, his covenant with
Israel and his election of the people seem to lose their significance. Yet Scripture affirms that the covenant will be valid forever
and that the Torah is given as an eternal order. In Romans 9–11
Paul defends both the new and the old orders of salvation, but
the attempt to do justice to both inevitably ends up in contradictions. In chapter 11 Paul wants to establish continuity, since God's
trustworthiness demands it, but the logic of his idea of salvation
speaks against it. In the olive tree parable (11:17–24), Paul talks as
if his church were a mainstream synagogue, with some new proselytes, from which a few apostates have been expelled. The social
reality was quite different: to speak in the language of the parable,
almost all old branches had been "cut off" and a very small number of new branches from a "wild olive tree" had been "grafted"
onto the old tree.

The question of inconsistency

Interpretations that assume that Paul was inconsistent have been
hotly debated for a quarter century now; they do not enjoy great
popularity among Pauline scholars. They are often said to attri-
bute nonsense to Paul. Yet attempts to deny inconsistency largely
boil down to giving it a different name. Such attempts include
development theories (which openly assume contradictions
between different letters), a distinction between the coherent

theme of Paul's gospel and its case-by-case application, or a distinction between practical aims and argumentative strategies. The effect is the same: Paul is found consistent only if the interpreter knows how to tell the coherent kernel from the unimportant husk.

Pauline scholars tend to argue that we should conclude that Paul was inconsistent only as a last resort. But why should this be so? Theologians are not at all reluctant to find inconsistencies even in "good" thinkers when they discuss the work of other theologians. Behind many criticisms of the inconsistency thesis lurks religious anxiety. As Douglas Moo openly states, it is important to find "coherence in Paul's argument if his theology is ultimately to inform our own perspectives and behavior." He asks, "Why should I take seriously the opinions of someone who is himself so confused that he contradicts himself in the space of fifteen hundred words [Rom 9–11] on a matter central to these chapters?" (p. 240). It is difficult not to see in such concerns a residue of the old doctrine of inspiration, if not of inerrancy. Do not the attempts to find in Paul coherence at all costs betray a kind of docetism? Real humans, including leading theologians, *are* often inconsistent and may well contradict themselves!

It is fair to demand that an interpreter try to "understand" Paul as far as possible—and yet one should not try excessively hard, for Paul's is but one stance in a conflict situation. I find "fair play" all-important in biblical study, that is, the taking seriously of the fact that we are listening to *one* party in a conflict in which the others remains mute. Responsible scholarship must try to do justice both to Paul and to those who disagreed with him. It is likely that every side had some understandable concerns. Nascent Christianity was a religion with conflicting convictions and we need to do justice to this diversity. It was not only persons and groups who were in conflict; the struggle between tradition and innovation also took place in the mind and heart of Paul, a controversial Jew with conflicting convictions.

There are different ways of taking a person seriously. Why couldn't we embrace Paul as a discussion partner rather than as an authority? Rather than taking any of Paul's statements as direct answers to our questions, it might be helpful to look to his *struggle* as a potential example for our situation as well, when embracing cultural pluralism is imperative, even if the outcome of his struggle may not seem intellectually successful. Paul is wrestling with his sacred tradition in light of his new experience (positively, the living together of different ethnic groups in his churches; negatively, the rejection of his message by most Jews). We, too, have to make sense of our traditions in light of *our* experience which includes the necessity of a critical approach to all traditions.

Chapter Three

Spotlight on Saint Paul

James A. Veitch

The trouble we have with the Apostle Paul is that he is *Saint*
Paul. A saint is a figure of respect, veneration and of awe
and this can conceal pathways to the truth. Saints are exceptional
human beings, persons of virtue and goodness who have become
entitled to the veneration of the faithful because of the reputation they have gathered for themselves during their lifetime. In
death they become untouchable or sacred, according to one dic-
tionary, attaining "through holy deeds or behavior an especially
exalted place in heaven entitling them to veneration."

Once granted this status it is extremely difficult to treat these
persons normally. Saints are human, in a sense more human than
the rest of us. But they are less than divine, in-between sorts of
creatures, lower than the angels and yet high enough to speak on
behalf of Almighty God. It follows that what a saint says must be
accepted at face value. It must be taken on trust and be believed.
For if saints stand closer to God than the rest of us, then it is
inconceivable that they would ever stretch the truth or tell a lie.

In one sense the problem we have with Saint Paul is similar
to that which we have with Jesus. Both are elusive figures of history who have become hidden in the folds of human piety and

The Fourth R 12,2 (1999), pp. 3–8

devotion, and encased in doctrine and belief; they are fragile figures who plead for protection. Their words have been reverently
placed in the pages of a holy book and decisions of authoritative
ecumenical church councils have given these words unchallenge-
able plausibility. Both have become immortalized in the psyche
of the world-wide community of faith—the church—that owes
its existence to these two figures. One is divine, the other a high-
ranking saint.

Turn the spotlight of the historical principle onto either Jesus
or Paul and it threatens to shatter the delicate figures into a thousand argumentative pieces. So these figures must be shielded from
the light to protect their divinity and saintliness. The church is
probably no more interested in a truly historical Paul than in an
authentically historical Jesus. To discover the truth about either—
let alone declare a no holds-barred, uncensored version of it—
threatens and intimidates the church and its congregations.

The Jesus Seminar and others have taken on the task of shin-
ing light on Jesus of Nazareth, and we have discovered not the
plastic figure of the liturgy and creed but a historical individual.
Now it is time to turn that same historical light on the church's
greatest saint—the Apostle Paul. We begin by looking back to the
nineteenth-century beginnings of this search and to the scholars
who have since taken on the task.

Exposing Paul to Historical Analysis

If it was Herman Reimarus (1694–1768) who at the close of
the eighteenth century posed the questions that have shaped the
debates about Jesus for two hundred years, then it was F. C. Baur
(1792–1860) in the nineteenth century who set the direction
of the search for a genuine Paul. Baur shifted the emphasis from
theology to history and tried to penetrate behind the smoke-
screen of the sainthood of Paul to the real individual. His first
essay about Paul, "The Christ Party in the Corinthian Church,"
was published in 1831; his two-volume major study, *Paul, His
Life and Works,* was published in German in 1845 (and in English
in 1875). Baur maintained that the historical Paul could only be
detected in the clash that occurred between Gentile and Jewish

Christianity. Paul represented the first of these strands; Peter the friend of Jesus, and the other friends together with James, the brother of Jesus, represented the second.

Attempts to mediate between these opposing parties are reflected in the gospels and letters of the New Testament. Those stories belong to the second and third stages in the development of early Christianity. According to Baur, there was no point in taking seriously the *Acts of the Apostles* as a record of Paul's actual life story, for it bore the stamp of this later mediation. Instead, Baur concentrated on the letters attributed to Paul and sorted these into groups according to their *tendency* or direction of argument. From his analysis Baur concluded Paul wrote only the letters to the Galatians, Corinthians and Romans.

His peers were taken by surprise and so was the church of his day. If these letters were accepted as the only genuine letters that still exist from the mind, if not the pen, of the historical Paul, then the person who emerges would be very different from the Paul of the church's thinking and teaching. Alarm bells began to ring. If becoming historical meant encountering the Paul of F. C. Baur, then the historical path should be rejected. The church had too much to lose in credibility. So much of what the church had become was regularly traced back to the influence of *Saint* Paul. If this origin were found to be historically suspect then the church's power and influence would be undermined. Better that scholars and theologians stay with theology and keep away from history except in so far as the historical could be used to support the theological. Not surprisingly, Baur faced sharp criticism as the church held him at arm's length. But he had opened Pandora's box: the study of Paul would never be the same again.

The Central Questions

Five key questions came out of Baur's work:

1. What was the relationship between Paul and Jesus? In particular what did Paul actually know about the historical figure and was he really interested in him?
2. What was the relationship between Paul and the family and the friends of Jesus?

3. Who were Paul's actual opponents, those he had in mind
   when he wrote his letters?
4. What sort of Jew was Paul and what was his relationship
   to the Judaisms of his day; what kind of Judaism influenced
   his thinking the most?
5. What was the core of his thinking, the organizing principle
   around which he grouped all his ideas and that he thought
   essential and significant for the lives of his listeners and
   readers?

For nearly 170 years these questions have been debated but
surprisingly not resolved. One of the reasons for this has been
the persistence in trying to resolve these matters theologically
and not historically. To continue to try to resolve the questions
theologically is to give tacit support to the traditional view the
church has taken of Paul. It is in fact to go round in circles.
Baur's key questions are raised, discussed, modified or rebutted
theologically without much progress being made. To set out to
resolve these questions historically is to risk destabilizing this
view of Paul, for any re-thinking which appears to be demanded
by Baur's questions also raises the fundamental question of the
origins of the church and of Christianity. These questions the
church may be willing to discuss theologically, but is still unwill-
ing to face historically and critically.

Enter Albert Schweitzer

Nearly a century ago Albert Schweitzer trailed the historical Jesus
through all the twists and curves of a hundred years of searching
and scholarly debate in order to catch a glimpse of his quarry.
The shadow that eventually fell across the path Schweitzer pur-
sued revealed an alarming end-of-the-world doomsday figure. It
was quite unlike the figure embedded in the Sunday liturgy and
found in the bread and wine of the mass and the Eucharist. For
this Jesus the end of the world was imminent. Obsessed with the
end of the world, Schweitzer's Jesus died believing that in his
death the end will arrive. Such a Jesus has a persona like none
other. Here is a tragic, disillusioned, savior-like figure who dies to
put his people on side with God as history speeds to its climatic
moment of destruction.

It is one of the oddest quirks in twentieth-century religious history that Schweitzer's apocalyptic, eschatological prophet figure, whom he thought so unattractive, has become the figure the church now venerates. Successive world wars, many smaller civil wars and conflicts, and extraordinary levels of social disjunction in a century of jarring change have made Schweitzer's Jesus a meaningful figure for a church in decline and retreat. Having got over the shock of Schweitzer's work on Jesus, the church plucked this portrait out of its context and began to read the New Testament as if it said exactly what Schweitzer had concluded.

Six years after publishing his major book on Jesus, Schweitzer saw *Paul and His Interpreters* into print. In it he says:

Anyone who deals with the teaching and the life and work of Jesus, and offers any kind of new reading of it, ought not to stop there, but must be held under obligation to trace, from the standpoint at which he has arrived, the pathway leading to the history of dogma. Only in this way can it be clearly shown what his discovery is worth. *(Paul and His Interpreters,* p. v)

The link was clear. When the work on Jesus was finished there was more to do, and the first candidate was the apostle Paul, key to the origins of Christianity and the church. Schweitzer set out to do for Paul what he had done for Jesus. He followed the figure through all the twists and turns of the nineteenth-century scholarly debate and wrote:

If the view adopted at the close of my Quest of the Historical Jesus is sound then the teaching of Jesus does not in any of its aspects go outside the Jewish world, . . . but represents a . . . perfected version of the contemporary Apocalyptic. . . .
    Therefore the Gospel is at its starting point exclusively Jewish-eschatological. *(Paul and His Interpreters,* p. ix)

In 1931, he followed with another book: *The Mysticism of Paul the Apostle.* Schweitzer was sure that Paul was not the Hellenizer of Christianity, though, he admitted, Paul's ideas did make it easier for others to transform his thinking into this genre *(Mysticism of Paul,* p. ix). Schweitzer did however believe that apocalyptic eschatology was central to an understanding of Paul's theology.

In this respect there was a continuum between Jesus and Paul. What Jesus had not achieved in his lifetime Paul was able to put in motion for him. It is not therefore surprising that Schweitzer's Paul soon became the standard portrait for theologian, biblical scholar, and preacher, and in time the influence of his thinking trickled down into the pews and the Sunday school room. Schweitzer's influence on the twentieth-century Protestant church membership has been quite remarkable.

Rudolf Bultmann on stage

In his *Theology of the New Testament* (2 volumes 1948, English 1951 and 1953, English 1955) Rudolf Bultmann reinterpreted Paul's first-century thinking into the existentialist language of the philosopher Martin Heidegger, so that it could make sense to the post-war generation he addressed. In the proclamation of the gospel God's presence is encountered and those who experience this presence are called to decide for or against a life of faith. If they say "yes," then they are "justified by their faith" and put alongside God.

What was, according to Schweitzer, an end of time happening becomes a reality experienced in the present moment. The believer who experiences the presence of God by saying yes as a response to the proclamation of the gospel is anticipating a meeting that would traditionally be expected at the end of life, or at the end of history. In such a response the believer experiences the free gift of God's righteousness.

This was a perfectly understandable reinterpretation of Pauline Christianity for all who had experienced the savagery and brutality of the Second World War and who had in the process lost sight of the presence of God in the stories about Jesus. In spite of the Lutheran and Germanic overtones of his thinking, Bultmann had re-opened the debate about Jesus and Paul and had again raised questions about the motivating core of Paul's thinking. He still believed that core to be the idea of justification by faith.

Bultmann's contribution was his reinterpretation of eschatology from something still to happen at the end of history to something that can really happen in the present moment. Others however were to modify or reject this view, as the church's biblical scholars, particularly in Germany, began to slowly recover from the catastrophe of war. In many ways Bultmann was still engaging in the debates of the nineteenth century and responding to Schweitzer. He too was a theologian who addressed the church and its immediate needs. In order to see Paul clearly another angle of vision had to be found. The real breakthrough in the understanding of Paul's thinking happened when scholars began to explore the nature of the Jewish world within which Paul lived and thought.

W. D. Davies and a new direction

In *Paul and Rabbinic Judaism* published in 1948, W. D. Davies wrote,

> Paul was a practising Jew who never ceased to insist that his gospel was first to the Jews, who also expected Jewish-Christians to persist in their loyalty to the Torah of Judaism, and who assigned to the Jews in the Christian no less than in the pre-Christian dispensation a place of peculiar importance. (p. 321)

Although it had never been doubted that Paul was a Jew, Davies was the first scholar to persist in emphasizing the significance of his Jewishness for understanding his thinking. "A Paul who when he became a Christian had ceased to be a Jew would not be the Paul that we know," Davies provocatively added (pp. 321–22). The Paul of Davies brings Judaism to its fulfilment with the founding of the church. Paul's Christianity was the new Torah, the new Exodus. What he ushered in was the messianic age of Jewish expectation. Paul's meeting with the risen Christ had made all the difference.

According to Davies, Paul was a Jew whose allegiance was to Jesus—another Jew—and to the God whom the latter revealed. He remained a Jew, though his commitment to the way of Jesus gave his Judaism a new dimension and significance. Drawing upon "concepts derived from Rabbinic Judaism" Paul reworked his Judaism and, in the process, Christianity and the church emerged.

Here we have a picture of Jesus and Paul cheek by jowl in the founding of Christianity joined together by their Judaism, with Paul seeing in the implications of what Jesus said and did the potential for a new form of Judaism. Here is a Paul who grasps the significance of the life, death and resurrection of Jesus for faith in God, and who turns that historical figure into a divine figure—a Christ-like messianic figure crucial for human salvation and, in the course of time, an object of worship.

Davies' achievement was to anchor Paul's Christianity firmly into its Jewish foundations and heritage, and in the process to open up dialogue with post-holocaust Judaism.

E. P. Sanders and re-defining Paul's Judaism

It took some time for the implications of Davies' Paul to be redrawn, but eventually E.P. Sanders, in three publications, explored in more detail the Jewish context for the thinking of Paul. He began in 1977 with *Paul and Palestinian Judaism* and followed this study with *Paul, the Law and the Jewish People* (1983) and *Paul* (1991). Unlike his predecessor and mentor W D. Davies, Sanders placed Paul into the context of Palestinian Judaism and suggested that Paul affirmed this form of Judaism as a valid path of salvation. God gave the Torah to the Jewish people and in Jesus the Jew he brought salvation to the world. Sanders' Jesus reaches the conclusion that the salvation the Jews knew and had experienced in their long history was incomplete. The story of Jesus the Jew, the Christ, completes this story. (But this is in fact the problem with Sanders: the term Christ effectively takes Jesus out of the world of Judaism and makes of him a different person than he was.)

Sanders' Paul stands in continuity with Jesus. He too is a Jewish figure influenced by the same sort of Judaism as Jesus. He was once a Pharisee. But importantly Paul is critical of Judaism and seeks to reinterpret it as he believes Jesus did. In Sanders, the eschatological emphasis of Schweitzer and of Bultmann has weakened, and Davies' emphasis on Jesus' Jewishness has been modified. Sanders' work was hailed as a refreshing breakthrough in Pauline scholarship. He had raised historical questions about Paul and his context without destabilizing the exiting portrait of Paul.

The Pauline Autobahn

Many scholars have worked on Paul. In Germany the names of Ernst Käsemann, Gunther Bornkamm, Dieter Georgi, Gerd Lüdemann (a Fellow of the Jesus Seminar), Peter Stuhlmacher,

Hans Dieter Betz, and Gerd Theissen stand out, as does that of
Heikki Räisänen from Scandanavia. In Britain F. F. Bruce, C. K.
Barrett, C. E. B. Cranfield, J. D. G. Dunn, Francis Watson and N. T.
Wright are important influences. In Israel it is Jerome Murphy-
O'Conner. In the United States, Krister Stendahl, J. Christiaan
Beker, Wayne Meeks, Richard Hays and Robert Jewett have been
associated with innovative studies. A new book by Jesus Seminar
Fellow John White suggests a fresh approach. There has been
and still is plenty of traffic on the freeway. Theologically, Pauline
scholarship is at the center of the church's search for identity, and
a breakthrough like that of Sanders opens new dimensions and
overturns outmoded shibboleths. Except for the idiosyncratic
contribution of Hyam Maccoby, the work of Jewish scholars,
among them Samuel Sandmel, Alan Segal and Daniel Boyarin
run in parallel to that of Sanders.

All current Pauline specialists emphasize the Jewishness of
Paul and his continuity with Jesus (but see the article by Gregory
Jenks in *Problems in Understanding the Apostle Paul,* a companion
volume to be published as Jesus Seminar Guide, vol. 6, in which
he shows that Paul hardly knew the historical Jesus). Paul is under
the influence of Palestinian Judaism and he is a Pharisee. He is
not a product of the Hellenistic Judaism of the Roman Empire
as nineteenth- and early twentieth-century scholars thought.
However, his thinking does move on beyond Palestinian Judaism.
He pushes out the boundaries of the Judaisms he knows, and
according to Christian scholars this means he has moved outside
Judaism into what has become known as Christianity. And once
outside he spends time in his letters trying to relocate himself
religiously while remaining in dialogue with the Judaism that he
has moved beyond.

Daniel Boyarin, however, takes a slightly different direction. In
A *Radical Jew,* he wishes to claim the study of Paul as "an inte-
gral part of the study of Judaism in the Roman period." Paul's
letters, he argues, are "extremely precious documents for Jewish
studies, the spiritual biography of a first-century Jew" (pp. 1–2).
Although Paul died believing that he was a Jew outside Judaism,
Boyarin suggests that he was a Jew to the end of his days. Paul, he
says, was a "Jewish cultural critic" who produced a proposal for
the radical reform of the Judaism and the Jewish culture that he

knew well. He was an internal critic of Jewish culture. His letters
are the record of a public discussion and debate about the inner
meaning and long term significance of key aspects of this culture.
If his ideas were used to start Christianity and the church then
others took those ideas and re-worked them. Others have suggested that Paul was a Pharisee, but a Pharisee in a category all its
own.

The traffic on the autobahn confusingly moves in different
directions and we are back to the questions of F. C. Baur without
much progress!

Where to Now?

The emphasis on the Jewishness of Paul (and of Jesus) is laudable
and understandable. After treating the Jews with an astonishing
depth of hatred for centuries, Christians discovered in the mid-
twentieth century the tragedy of the holocaust in which they
had played a part. To accept without qualification the significance
and the implications of the Jewishness of Jesus was as essential as
it was necessary. But Paul introduced a new set of problems. In
the light of first-century and modem Judaism who was this man?
It was time to put aside theology and to explore some answers
historically. Is it possible that the twisted and tortured relationship between Judaism and Paul, as set out in (at least) the letters
of Galatians and Romans, has its origins not in Paul's Jewishness
but elsewhere? In spite of nearly two centuries of debate the key
questions raised by Baur continue to haunt Pauline scholarship.

The Jesus Seminar has sought to rigorously excavate the gospels in a search for the historical Jesus, in response to the questions raised by Hermann Reimarus. A similar approach now
needs to be taken by the Seminar as it initiates an honest and
open search for the Paul of history. In the long run this cannot
be achieved without taking up the key questions of F C. Baur
and applying the historical-critical method to the study of the
whole Pauline corpus.

This will automatically include a new and a detailed study
of the relationship of the Book of Acts to the actual letters of
the Paul of history. It will also involve identifying the actual letters written by Paul or dictated to a secretary. Only when these

tasks have progressed can attention turn to a study of Paul's own ideas set within the context of the Jewish and Hellenistic world in which he moved. It may then be possible to be clear about Paul's own theology, and one piece of the puzzle of the origins of Christianity and the church will be in place, leaving the way open for the study of what happened in the following one hundred years.

Chapter Four

The Second Founder of Christianity

John L. White

W hen liberal nineteenth-century German scholars tried to recover the historical Jesus, they often accused Paul of being the principal corrupter of Jesus' identity, claiming he created the doctrinal system that changed Jesus into a divine being. For example, in his book, *What is Christianity?*, Adolf Harnack said Paul transplanted Christianity from its Jewish origin in Jesus to Greek pagan soil. By altering Jesus' gospel about God's coming kingdom into the message that Jesus himself was a divine savior, Paul opened the door to a range of Greco-Roman ideas and practices.

Harnack rejected Paul's Hellenizing additions and located the church's true essence in Jesus' moral teachings. According to Harnack, Jesus did not call attention to his own status but taught enduring truths about God and what he expected of people, such as God's universal fatherhood and the brotherhood of humanity. If adopted, his principles would result in worldwide peace (= God's kingdom on earth). By contrast, Paul taught that humanity was incapable of living the benevolent life and said it had to depend on the salvation God had effected by his divine son, Jesus.

The Fourth R 12,5–6 (1999), pp. 3–10

Although twentieth-century scholars came to dispute
Harnack's picture of Jesus as an optimistic teacher and concluded
that he, as well as Paul, believed in the need of God's external
intervention, Paul's message often continued to be set in opposition to that of Jesus. My own judgment, however, is that Paul
was just as concerned with a new and paradoxical conception of
God as Jesus was. Theology was far more important to Paul than
christology (the idea of Jesus as Christ). Thus, unlike Harnack and
modern scholars who think Jesus' divinity and sacrificial death are
the key to Paul's religious system, I am convinced Paul's root idea
of God was fundamentally like that of Jesus. That conception of
God led both to become social radicals.

The Non-Traditional Jesus and the Traditional Dogmatic Paul?

The liberal picture of Jesus as an optimistic teacher came under
attack early in the twentieth century, when Albert Schweitzer
argued that Jesus believed the world was so unjust that God
would destroy it shortly and create a new order. According to
Schweitzer, when that did not happen, Jesus concluded he himself must die to make the end arrive. Although Schweitzer concluded that the ongoing flow of history proved Jesus was a tragic
and mistaken apocalyptic preacher, the church and a majority of
American scholars still venerate the apocalyptic Jesus.

Despite the ongoing popularity of apocalyptic ideas, it became
increasingly clear to many scholars by the mid-twentieth century
that it was no longer feasible to say Jesus predicted the literal end
of the world. Members of the Westar Institute's Jesus Seminar,
for example, are convinced the earliest stage of the Jesus tradition consisted of his parables, and the most authentic parables
nowhere announce a cataclysmic end of history. Reflecting the
majority opinion of the Jesus Seminar, Robert Funk argues in
his book, *Honest to Jesus,* that Jesus did not announce the end
of the world but was a sage who taught God was already making himself present in the everyday experiences of life. This does
not mean Funk or the Jesus Seminar have returned to Adolf
Harnack's idea of Jesus as a teacher of universal maxims. To the

contrary, there is broad agreement that Jesus' folk teaching was of a paradoxical kind and was anything but practical in the conventional sense.

Funk also reflects the majority opinion when he contrasts Jesus' message with that of Paul and proceeds to describe Paul as the precursor of Christianity's fourth-century dogmatic creeds. I agree that Paul did not use Jesus' Palestinian images to talk about God and that he recast his message in Greco-Roman terms. But, for several reasons, I cannot agree that Paul corrupted Jesus' idea of God or that he was an advocate of religious dogmatism.

First, we cannot set Paul's viewpoint directly over against Jesus, because Paul did not create Hellenistic Christianity (= the Greek-speaking Jewish church) but was himself a convert to its perspective. In contrast to Palestinian Christianity (= the Hebrew-speaking Jewish church), Hellenistic Christianity was granting non-Jews (Gentiles) admittance to Judaism without requiring traditional entry requirements such as circumcision, prescribed dietary rules and obedience to Moses' law. Many Jews found this interpretation offensive and destructive of Jewish identity. In fact, prior to his conversion, Paul himself found this form of Judaism aberrant and he tried to destroy it,

> . . . you have heard of my former life in Judaism, how I persecuted the church of God violently and tried to destroy it; and I advanced in Judaism beyond many of my own age among my people, so extremely zealous was I for the traditions of my fathers.
> (Gal 1:13–14; see Phil 3:3–7)

Later, after becoming a convert of the Hellenistic Church, he did, in fact, justify its aberrant conversion of Gentiles and become its most articulate defender.

Second, it is not accurate to draw a direct line from Paul to fourth-century creeds which confess belief in Jesus' divinity. In fact, Paul's idea of God's paradoxical elevation of a condemned criminal (Jesus) hardly fits either Jewish or Greco-Roman conventions. His idea of God's comparable elevation of Gentile converts of lowly status is equally antithetical to social convention. Paul advocated an enlarged and paradoxical idea of God and, much more than most in his day, was an advocate of social egalitarianism.

How, then, did Paul come to be identified as the father of the church's later orthodoxy? The answer begins with the observation that he was, in fact, a source of two different streams of Christian tradition—dogmatic orthodoxy on the one hand and "heretical" opposition to convention on the other hand.

In his letters Paul refers metaphorically to the Hellenistic Church's Gentile converts as a freeborn family household. In this fictive family, God is the spiritual father, Jesus is the designated heir and non-Jewish converts are divine offspring in relation to God and siblings in relation to one another. By calling converts God's people, Paul extended Jewish ethnic ideals of special status to Gentiles and, by admitting the freedman class and slaves into this family as full members, Paul altered Greco-Roman ideas of class status and the definition of family. However, when Paul's ideas of the church as a fictive family were appropriated by Colossians, Ephesians and the Pastoral Epistles, these New Testament representatives reintroduced the hierarchical values originally associated with the Greco-Roman household. Thus, Colossians and Ephesians both contain traditional household codes which direct wives to be subject to husbands, children to be obedient to parents and slaves to be submissive to masters (Col 3:18–4:1; Eph 5:22–6:9; see 1 Tim 2:8–3:13; Titus 1:5–2:10).

In contrast to this view, Marcionites, Valentinians and other heretical groups called "gnostic" (= true knowledge) Christians used Paul's family metaphors to refute and undermine social, ethnic and religious convention. They focused on non-hierarchical emphases in Paul's description of the church as fictive family, underscoring the egalitarian relationship of family members exhibited in such Pauline imagery as "brethren" *(adelphoi)*. Thus, in a study of the gnostic Gospel of Thomas, Stephen Patterson shows that Thomas, like Paul, opposed the circumcision of Gentiles (see Thom 53), opposed the need to observe kosher food laws (Thom 14:4–5), and defended the right of women to full participation and leadership in the Church (Thom 114). The appropriation of Paul by Thomas and other representatives of the "gnostic" church indicate Paul could be used to refute orthodoxy as much as to enshrine it.

Which one of the two streams understood Paul better? I will not answer the question absolutely, but am convinced the gnostic attack on convention found a valid basis of support in Paul.

Central Questions

We now turn to the questions that scholars have customarily raised to assess Paul's relation to Jesus and to situate Paul's place in the development of early Christianity. Before proceeding to the questions, I want to summarize what has been said thus far about Paul's relation to Jesus' theological perspective. I have argued that Paul, like Jesus, was possessed by a new idea of God that drove him to defy major Jewish taboos and to trespass many Greco-Roman conventions. Moreover, Paul used metaphors to describe God's unexpected activities in relation to the world in a way that is fundamentally analogous to Jesus' paradoxical way of talking about God in parables. Although Jesus did not announce the world's cataclysmic end, his counter-cultural ideas about God were nonetheless "earth shattering." Likewise, the way Paul described God's new creation as originating with the resurrection of a condemned criminal and as being formed of non-Jews is equally striking. Both Paul and Jesus were social radicals in a fundamental sense.

Jim Veitch in his essay "Spotlight on St. Paul" (see chap. 3) identifies five key questions arising from F. C. Baur's nineteenth-century study of Paul that are still relevant for determining the nature of Paul's relation to Jesus and for locating his role in Christianity's early development. I reformulate Veitch's wording slightly:

1. What did Paul know about the historical Jesus and was he really interested in him?
2. What was the relationship between Paul and the family and friends of Jesus?
3. Who were Paul's actual opponents when he wrote his letters?
4. What sort of Jew was Paul and what was his relation to the Judaisms of his day?

5. What was the core of Paul's thinking, the organizing principle around which he grouped all his ideas?

In many respects, these questions are interrelated and cannot
be answered independently. Nonetheless, I will discuss them sepa-
rately with the exception of numbers 2 and 4, which are con-
nected in my view and must be taken up together.

What did Paul know about the historical Jesus?

Paul states only a few details about the historical Jesus. For example, he cites Jesus' command that a married couple ought not to
separate or divorce (1 Cor 7:10) and he says the Lord's Supper
tradition was inaugurated by Jesus on the night of his betrayal (1
Cor 11:23–25). For the most part, however, Paul prefers to refer
to Jesus' life only in broad terms.

Although Paul had a special interest in Jesus' death, he did not
concern himself with it primarily as a sacrificial atonement for
other people's sins. Rather, before and after conversion, Paul was
struck by the shamefulness of the death from a Jewish legal viewpoint (see Gal 3:10–13; see also 1 Cor 1:17–25). Thus, he justifies
his earlier persecution of Hellenistic Christians on the basis of
his loyalty to tradition and clearly implies the Hellenistic Church
was breaking the law and destroying the foundations of Jewish
community (see Gal 1:13f.; Phil 3:2–6; 2 Cor 11:20–12:10). That
lawlessness originated with its founder, Jesus, who himself was
condemned by Jewish law. Paul reflects this conviction in Gal
3:13:

Christ redeemed us from the curse of the law by becoming a
curse for us—for it is written, "Cursed is everyone who hangs on
a tree."

As a Pharisaic interpreter, Paul knew from Deuteronomy
(21:22–23) that anyone who committed a crime punishable by
death, and whose corpse was desecrated by later being hanged on
a tree, was cursed by God. Since Jesus was convicted of a crime
punishable by death, and since his execution fit the biblical pattern of being hanged up for public derision, it was clear he was
cursed. Moreover, by admitting Gentiles into the Greek-speaking
Jewish Church without requiring typical entry requirements,
Jesus' Hellenistic followers were keeping his lawlessness alive

and the Jewish community was being contaminated. According to Deuteronomy (21:23), an accursed criminal must be taken down and buried the same day of his execution lest he sterilize the communal soil on which life depended. By persecuting the Hellenistic Church Paul tried to lay Jesus' curse to rest for good.

Then, unexpectedly, he had a vision from God of the resurrected Jesus (Gal 1:15f.). He reasoned that, since Jesus was alive, he was not cursed but vindicated and blessed by God. He was the Christ proclaimed by the lawless Hellenistic church! How could this be?

What was clear to Paul was that Mosaic law was not fully able to explain the ways of God. In fact, just the opposite: God had blessed the very person who had been condemned and cursed by the law. Far from rushing to some positive evaluation of Jesus' trust in God which warranted approval, however, Paul first had to work through the negative and paradoxical facts of the situation. Gentiles were being admitted into God's community without being required to abide by major Jewish laws—such as those regarding kosher and circumcision, and someone executed by the law had become the means of facilitating the inclusion. Paul felt forced to make sense of this nonsense in Jewish terms and thus he was driven back to the tradition for an analogy. His answer is taken up in the following section.

What sort of Jew was Paul and what was his relation to the family and friends of Jesus?

Although Paul was a Greek-speaking Jew, he was a member of the Pharisaic sect and not inclined prior to conversion to move toward a Greco-Roman understanding of Judaism. Even when he became an advocate of the Greek-speaking (Hellenistic) Jewish Church he had neither the secular leanings of Josephus nor the philosophical bent of Philo. It was not Greek culture *per se* that caused his new Hellenizing view, but a paradoxical experience of the risen Jesus. This was what made him broaden his idea of God. The change was radical enough that it is not hard to understand how some interpreters have concluded that Paul was a Gentile prior to conversion and not a Jew.

When faced with the task of reconciling God's adoption of Gentiles—as Gentiles—to be his people, and with finding some

way of making sense of God's choice of Jesus to be his messianic
son, Paul found a precursor in the biblical Abraham. Like Jesus
and lawless Gentile converts, Abraham had neither the birth nor
the achieved status to qualify him to father God's people. He
had to receive his status through spiritual adoption. For many
diaspora Jews (= Jews outside the Jewish homeland), including
Philo, Abraham was an ideal prototype of would-be proselytes
(= Gentile converts). Leaving homeland and family was a potent
metaphor for Gentiles, even if not literally true. Because of what
Gentiles had to give up, by way of family and ethnic identity,
Philo could describe them as worthy of special recognition within Judaism.

Like Philo, Paul argued that Gentiles had first-class standing
as God's people. Unlike Philo and most Jewish representatives,
however, he did not make their status depend on submission to
circumcision and other Jewish admission requirements. Gentile
acceptability, as in the case of Abraham before circumcision
(Rom 3:9–12; see Gal 3:6–11, 17), derived from simple trust in
God's power to effect what he promised. Thus, for Paul, Gentile
converts were not an aberrant form of offspring in God's community but, exactly like Abraham and Jesus, were adopted as
spiritual offspring in spite of deficiencies under Jewish law. The
identical lineage of Abraham, Jesus and Gentile converts is stated
in Gal 3:14f.:

> Christ redeemed us from the curse of the law by becoming
> a curse for us—for it is written, "Cursed is everyone who
> hangs on a tree"—in order that in Christ Jesus the blessing
> of Abraham might come to the Gentiles, so that we might
> receive the promise of the Spirit through faith.

Paul makes it clear elsewhere that Jesus, and not Abraham's son
Isaac, was Abraham's true offspring (see Gal 3:16). This was so, not
only because God's promise to bless the nations (Gentiles) was
being effected through Abraham's promised seed, Jesus, but also
because the act of procreation effected in the case of Abraham
and Jesus was entirely analogous. Thus, Paul reads Jesus' death and
resurrection back into Isaac's birth out of Abraham and Sarah's
sterility. In Rom 4:17 Paul describes Isaac's conception explicitly
as God giving life to the dead: "who (that is, God) gives life to

the dead and calls into existence the things that do not exist."
Correspondingly, Paul interpreted Jesus' death and resurrection
according to the Abrahamic image of barrenness and conception.
The form of Jesus' execution (cursed under the law and a potential cause of sterility to others) corresponded to Abraham and
Sarah's barrenness. In the same vein, Jesus' resurrection is imaged
as the act of procreation that made him Abraham's promised heir
and God's messianic son:

> Now the promises were made to Abraham and to his off-
> spring (seed) . . . that is, to one person, who is Christ. (Gal
> 3:16)

The above explanation of Paul's experience of the resurrected
Jesus was not something he worked out after many years. It stood
at the beginning as authorization for his commission to be the
Apostle to the Gentiles. He makes it clear that as a Christian
convert he never advocated circumcision of Gentile converts
nor observance of kosher food laws which separated him from
table fellowship with them (in Galatians 1–2). Thus, he was never
a conservative Christian like James, the brother of Jesus, nor a
mediating convert like Peter. From the start, he was an advocate
of Gentile conversion without circumcision.

Consequently, the picture in Acts of Paul always beginning his
missionary activity among Jews in diaspora (Greek-speaking) synagogues is a fabrication. With the exception of Romans, a letter
written to a church that Paul did not found, all of his authentic
letters suggest the dominant makeup of his churches was Gentile.
Thus, the implication both in Acts and in many modern scholars
that Paul was a closet rabbi, who founded synagogue-like churches, is wrong. There may have been some Gentiles who earlier had
associated with synagogues in Paul's churches, but they were not
his primary audience.

Equally suspect is the view, largely derived from Acts, that
Paul's independent mission to Gentiles did not occur until over
half way through his missionary career. According to this view,
all of Paul's authentic letters were written in the last half of his
career, at a time when he wrote only to churches that he himself
had founded. In this case, I prefer the view (of John Knox, John
Hurd, Gerd Lüdemann, F. Stanley Jones and others) that Paul's

missionary work in Greece began as much as a decade earlier
than is commonly assumed. Moreover, I follow John Knox in
thinking Paul never worked as a junior partner under Barnabas
and the Antioch church. The texture of his rhetoric suggests he
founded Gentile churches without authorization from other
Christian leaders from the very start of his missionary career.

Who were Paul's actual opponents when he wrote his letters?

Many scholars suggest the coherence of thought in Paul's letters derived from a recurring problem with Judaizing critics. On
the other hand, recent scholars (among them Christiaan Beker,
Daniel Patte, and Norman Petersen) have argued the coherence
derives from Paul's own convictions. I agree with the latter group
that Paul's theological agenda was not determined by Jewish
opposition.

Paul's commitments certainly brought him into conflict with
Jewish traditionalists, but not nearly so much as is often assumed.
For example, though Acts says opposition to Paul in Thessalonica
was spearheaded by jealous Jews, Paul himself says his Thessa-
lonian converts were formerly pagans and implies that any hos-
tility against them came from fellow Gentiles (Acts 17:1ff.; for
example, see 1 Thess 1:4–10). Similarly, whereas Acts says jealous
Jews caused problems for Paul in Corinth, Paul says quarrelling
and dissension in the church arose out of jealous competitive-
ness of a Greek nature (Acts 18:1ff.; see 1 Cor 1:4ff.). To be sure,
Jewish-Christian outsiders caused problems at Corinth later,
boasting that they were more authentic apostles than Paul, since
they could work greater miracles. But, even in this case, Paul
makes the Corinthians share the blame by suggesting that they
were already inclined to prefer the self-commendation and glitzy
show of the "super" apostles over his own concern for the common good (see 2 Cor 10:1ff.).

Paul does launch an excessive attack on circumcision and circumcisers in Gal 5:2ff and in Phil 3:2f, but Judaism is less the
target than analogous pagan attractions. Paul uses the demeaning
picture of circumcisers as mutilators (Phil 3:2–3) as a ploy for
attacking the real target, the church's temptation to model itself
on pagan civic clubs, which gloried in their public service, but

which actually spent more time in socializing activities. Thus, Paul reminds converts their citizenship was of a heavenly nature and that Jesus was the role model of true citizenship (Phil 3:20). Though Paul is often accused of attacking Jewish practices in Romans, in fact, he attacked everyone—Gentile and Jew alike—who based status with God on self-won recognition. The true offspring of God was someone like Abraham, who put confidence in God and not in his own accomplishments (Rom 4:1ff.; see 2:25–29).

What was the Core of Paul's thinking, the organizing principle around which he grouped all his ideas?

As a result of God's revelation of the resurrected Jesus to Paul, Paul was driven to a new idea of God's identity. No longer could he think of God primarily as judge or lawgiver, even if the paradigm were enlarged to universal lawgiver. God's resurrection of Jesus forced Paul to find a different paradigm, one that could account for such paradoxical activity. Thus, as all of Paul's letters show, he understood God as creator, as that life-giving force that could bring fertility out of sterility, good out of bad, even life out of death. Because of the personal way he was struck by this revelation, Paul prefers to talk about God's creativity in terms of the procreativity of a father.

The idea of God as personal parent who effects spiritual procreation, pervades Paul's writings from his earliest to his last letter. The resurrected Jesus certainly had a temporal priority as God's "first-born" son in the new spiritual creation and, by virtue of temporal priority, he had the eldest son's correlative status as heir ("Lord") of God's family. Nonetheless, he was not the recipient of a singular, non-repeatable action that excluded a like experience for other spiritual siblings. Paul believed God effected a comparable experience of good over evil in his converts' lives as well as in Jesus'.

One more aspect of Paul's perspective remains to be reviewed: the implications of his idea of God for ethical conduct. Paul's critics allege that his idea of God undercut any valid basis of morality. According to this view, Paul believed humanity's sinfulness crippled it so badly that it was unable to obey God's laws and that its only recourse was to accept Jesus' sacrificial death on its behalf. This idea assumes that Paul never abandoned a legal idea of God, but merely substituted a forgiving judge who accepted the sacrifice of Jesus as atonement for human sin. In contrast with the idea of God as a Jewish lawgiver, Paul came to the more universal idea of God as a creator. To be sure, human creatures were still dependant on God as the source of regeneration but, once spiritual creation had been sparked, offspring had to "grow up" into the life-effecting character of their divine parent.

Four metaphors of the church in 1 Corinthians illustrate Paul's ethical view. Three are in chapters 3–4: the church as God's planted field (crop), the church as God's building (temple) and the church as God's family. A fourth image—the church as Christ's body—appears later in 1 Corinthians (see 1 Cor 6:15ff., 12:12ff.). All four images derive from the root idea of God as creator and all assume that God's life-giving benefits effect growth and progress. The idea of God as creator led Paul to nature's fertility as one source of images for expressing God's spiritual productivity. Thus, in 1 Cor 15:20, Jesus is described as the "first fruits" from the dead. In turn, Paul likens his Gentile converts to God's fertile field in 1 Cor 3:5–9. He makes it clear the field's full term growth (harvest) does not derive from the human farmers who tended it, whether Paul himself or Apollos, but productivity results only from subjecting selfish interests to the productive climatic conditions generated by God.

God was not only the creator of nature's fertility but also the generative power behind the creation of social institutions. Thus, Paul describes the church as a spiritually-generated family in 1 Cor 3:1–4 and again in 4:1ff. Paul argued that true relation to God would benefit the common good, in communal maturation and in social excellence. Paul's comparison of converts to members of a single human body (1 Cor 12:12–26) is a civic/political metaphor which Greeks like Plato and Aristotle had used to describe the interdependence of people of different social classes in the state. In the same way, Paul said the church was Christ's body and underscored community members' need, in the manner of Jesus, to perform acts that contributed to the common good rather than to individual glory.

Finally, though the reference to the church as a building in
1 Cor 3:10ff. seems initially not to fit the dynamic (biological)
nature of the three previous metaphors, even in this case Paul's
focus is not on the static edifice, but on the process of "building up." The building is truly God's temple when its walls "go
up" in harmony with the sacrificial foundation laid in Jesus.
Thus, though the image does not lend itself naturally to the idea
of harmony and growth found in the other three images, Paul's
emphasis on progress is similar.

Taken together, all four images suggest that spiritual offspring
must embody the positive life-begetting effects that characterize
their divine parent. By contrast, offspring must shun whatever
disrupts productivity, or causes chaos, disunity and destruction.
Such things are sterile, deadly and opposed to God. Paul uses
many other metaphors which are compatible with his root idea
of God, for they also describe activities—competing in athletic
competition, playing musical instruments, engaging in military
service, etc.—which evoke a successful and progressive outcome.

Concluding Reflections

Paul's idea of God as a power that reverses the Jewish law's
condemnation of Jesus and adopts non-Jews to be Abraham's
descendants corresponds to Jesus' table fellowship with "sinners"
and with his parable about a God who offers assistance through
a hated enemy of the Jew—the Samaritan. Both Jesus and Paul
had an unconventional and paradoxical idea of God's power to
reverse negative social circumstance. Most importantly, the new
social reality was not something awaiting future arrival, but was
already making its presence tangibly felt in the present. Because
Paul transposed Jesus' theological vision into a new ethnic key,
he may be justly described as the second founder of Christianity.
Nonetheless, there is good evidence that Paul's transplanted product was not in opposition to Jesus' perspective but supportive of
his root idea of God. Even Paul's near blasphemous description of
God's intimate parental association with his creation finds its parallel in Jesus' address to God as "Abba."

Chapter Five

Making Sense of Paul

Daryl D. Schmidt

The letters of the apostle Paul are again the subject of much scholarly debate. Paul's rhetorical style often requires the interpreter to read between the lines to discern what the real issues are. To get a good sense of Paul's argument, the interpreter must read Paul with this dominant question in mind:

What problem was Paul trying to solve?

How one describes Paul's solution depends significantly on how this question is answered. For a growing number of scholars, this question must be answered in terms that fit the world in which Paul lived, the Jewish intellectual world of the Diaspora, that is, the world outside of Roman Palestine.

Paul lived in an urban center in Asia Minor. For Greek-speaking intellectuals the highest cultural value was universalism, the belief in the fundamental unity of humankind. For someone like Paul, this meant thinking about the human condition in global terms. The most effective analysis of "what's wrong with the world" would have to apply to everyone. The challenge, of

The Fourth R 15,2 (2002), pp. 9–14

course, is to offer a solution that matches the problem. Here is how many scholars now make sense of Paul's solution—and the problem he is trying to solve.

Problem: All humankind is in a state of decline.

Paul begins with the assumption that "we're all in this together," that the same condition applies to everyone and that condition is in a state of decline. In Paul's worldview, this rests on two irrefutable beliefs: everyone is accountable and God is impartial. First of all, there is only one God who will judge everyone on the same basis—Jew and non-Jew alike. This basic assertion of Jewish monotheism is captured in the creedal statement of Deut 6:4, often recited by Jews as a central affirmation of faith, called the Shema, after the first word in Hebrew. Paul echoes the Shema in Rom 3:30, Gal 3:20, and 1 Cor 8:4:

> Hear, O Israel! The Lord is our God, the Lord is one.

(The Gospel of Mark has Jesus recite this in conversation with a scholar, who comments, "and there is no other," to make explicit the monotheistic intent, Mark 12: 29–32). This is the God who will judge everyone. In exercising God's rightful judgment, God does not discriminate—again in the words of Scripture, reflected in Paul's argument in Rom 2:5, 11; Gal 2:6:

> The Lord your God is God supreme and Lord supreme,
> The awesome God, who shows no favor and takes no bribe.
>   (Deut 10:17)

Secondly, the comparable assumption from the human side is that we are all accountable for what we do. In the language of scripture: "God will repay each of us based on what we've done" (Ps 62:12; Prov 24:12). Paul uses this text in Rom 2:6 and 2 Cor 5:10. Paul thus affirms, "deeds matter." This would, of course, be true for everyone, with or without the Mosaic law.

These two principles become fundamental for Paul: parity—between Jew and non-Jew, and impartiality—on the part of God. These principles constitute God's very integrity (justice, righteousness, covenantal loyalty), which exists apart from the law (Rom 3:21). God was reliable—you could trust what God said—even before the time of Moses and the Mosaic law.

From his two basic assumptions, Paul draws two important corollaries regarding the scope of the problem he is describing. First of all, the universality of judgment means that "everyone has sinned" (Rom 3:23). This is Paul's summary of the human condition. The evidence is obvious to anyone willing to notice, as Paul is quite willing to point out in Rom 1:18–32, and it is also documented in scripture (Rom 3:9–20), especially the Psalms. Paul begins the documentation (Rom 3:10–12) with Psalm 14 (repeated in Psalm 53):

> Fools say to themselves, "There is no god."
>   Their deeds are corrupt; there is no one virtuous.
> God looks upon the human race,
>   To see if anyone even seeks God.
> Everyone has strayed and become corrupt,
>   There is no one virtuous—not one.

Equally important, God's impartiality means that observant Jews are not exempt. When Paul summarizes the evidence using Psalm 143, "no mortals will be acceptable (considered virtuous) to God," he edits it to add, "based on their distinctive ethnic practices" (Gal 2:16; Rom 3:20). Today we would consider this to be ethnic religious parochialism—the belief that God prefers one group's traditional customs over all others.

According to Paul's argument for universality, to allow any special conditions would nullify both principles of parity and impartiality. Paul then makes explicit the effect these assumptions have on evaluating his own tradition. The practice of the Mosaic customs does not affect either God's impartiality nor human accountability.

If the problem is described in universal terms, then the solution likewise must be applicable to everyone. Paul seeks a solution that can explain how God can provide salvation from the human situation, both to Jews and non-Jews alike, while remaining impartial.

Solution: God counts total trust as virtue.

The Mosaic law itself ironically provides the clue for Paul's solution, that God counts total trust as virtue, which Paul finds in the example of Abraham. Paul notes three crucial components in the sequence of the story of Abraham.

God makes a promise to Abraham:
I will make of you a great nation, and I will bless you;
All the nations will be blessed through you.
   (Gen 12:2, 3)

God reiterates the promise when Abraham points out that he is still childless in his old age:

Your offspring will be like the stars of the heavens. (Gen 15:5)

Abraham accepts God's word at face value:

Abraham trusted God and God considered him virtuous. (Gen 15:6)

Abraham's wife Sarah remains childless, even though Abraham fathers a child with Hagar, Sarah's maid. God renews the promise to Abraham, this time in a binding covenant, marked by circumcision (Gen 17:10–11).

This three-step sequence is treated by Paul as the definitive insight into God's plan of salvation: universal promise—trust—ethnic distinction.

The decisive moment in God's plan for salvation is Abraham's total trust in God's promise to him (Rom 4:3; Gal 3:6), which God in turn credits as an act of virtue, akin to God's own integrity—since indeed faithfulness is also one of God's traits, as Paul notes in 1 Cor 1:9; 10:13; 2 Cor 1:18:

Know that the Lord your God is God, a faithful God,
who keeps his covenant and mercy with those who love
God and keep the commandments
and renders judgment on those who reject God.
   (Deut 7:9–10)

God would be justified in rendering justice based only on deeds. Instead, God counts Abraham's trust as though it were virtue. For Paul this makes possible a whole new understanding for how God's promises are accomplished.

Paul focuses first on Abraham, emphasizing that Abraham was in fact a Gentile when God credited his trust as virtue—he was not yet circumcised (Rom 4:9–11). Circumcision was a symbol, after the fact, of Abraham's decisive act of total trust. Paul further notes the corollary that this credit is the equivalent of "the Lord not taking into account sin," quoting Ps 32:2 (Rom 4:8). In God's accounting system, trust counts against sin—even for Gentiles like Abraham.

Paul then makes the deduction that Abraham's act of trust can be a paradigm for everyone who has that kind of trust (Rom 4:24)—Jew and non-Jew alike. God's promise to Abraham is thus inherited by those who exhibit that kind of trust (Rom 4:16). In fact, these dual tracks thereby fulfill the promise itself that Abraham would be "the ancestor of many nations/Gentiles" (Gen 17:5, quoted in Rom 4:17). Indeed, this then fulfills the original promise made to Abraham that through him "all the nations will be blessed" (quoted in Gal 3:8).

Paul's solution accomplishes several of his important concerns:

1. It maintains God's integrity: God is one (as all Jews affirm), God keeps promises, God holds everyone accountable, God is impartial.
2. It allows for inclusion of the Gentiles (all other peoples) in God's plan of salvation, based on the vital role of Abraham—as a Gentile.
3. It recognizes total trust as the link between Abraham and other Gentile believers.

Results: Total trust brings life.

Abraham and Sarah, in their old age, were "good as dead" when new life came to them, an indication of what happens to those who totally trust that "God can do what God has promised" (Rom 4:19, 21). The ultimate act of such trust for Paul was Jesus' total trust in God, who "raised him from among the dead" (Rom 4:24; 8:11; Gal 1:1). As a result, the promise to Abraham that all humankind would be blessed through him is now fully available to everyone on the basis of trust (Gal 3:22). God's very integrity is linked to Jesus' total trust in God, who gives equal treatment to everyone who has that kind of trust, since God does not discriminate (Rom 3:22, 26).

Scripture provides Paul with a motto that links together these key concepts and becomes central in Paul's argument (Rom 1:17; Gal 3:11):

Those acceptable to God, based on total trust, will have life. (Hab 2:4)

This motto connects both Abraham and Jesus to every person who exhibits total trust. In fact, the whole process begins and ends with trust (Rom 1:17).

Paul also confidently edits another favorite text. He already read Ps 143:2 "no mortals will be acceptable [considered virtuous] to God," to mean, "based on their distinctive ethnic practices" (Rom 3:20). The fuller explanation for Paul is that mortals will be acceptable to God only through a total trust like that of Jesus, God's Anointed" (Gal 2:16).

The Mosaic law itself is not based on trust, since "those who observe its requirements will live by them" (Lev 18:5, quoted in Gal 3:12). As a result, it is not their distinctive ethnic practices that make people acceptable to God, rather it is their confidence in God's Anointed, who exemplified total trust.

Paul asks the Galatians a rhetorical question, which he surely thinks applies to all persons of faith: "Did you receive the spirit based on your distinctive ethnic practices or based on completely trusting what you heard?" (Gal 3:2, 5). The answer is provided by the story of Abraham.

Another way to talk about this same principle is the language of obedience. "One person's obedience made vindication possible for others," in the same way that "a single just act brought everyone acquittal and life" (Rom 5:18–19). Paul thus can describe his very mission as promoting "faithful obedience" (Rom 1:5). Whole-hearted obedience to this way of thinking shifts one's allegiance from sin to divine justice (Rom 6:16–17). For Paul the allegiance to the principle of trust means that the ritual of baptism amounts to sharing in the death of God's Anointed, Jesus, which of course anticipates sharing in his life as well (Rom 6:3–8; Gal 2:19–20).

The understanding Paul has achieved allows him to explain the death of Jesus as part of God's scheme. Paul lays out the argument from scripture in sequence in Galatians:

1. "Everyone who does not honor all the injunctions in the . . . law, by observing them, is accursed." (Deut 27:26, quoted in Gal 3:10)
2. This again confirms: "no one is acceptable to God" based on the law. (Gal 3:11, based on Ps 143:2)
3. Rather, "those acceptable, based on total trust, will have life." (Hab 2:4, quoted in Gal 3:11)
4. The law indeed is not based on trust: "those who observe its requirements will live by them." (Lev 18:5, quoted in Gal 3:12)
5. Because "anyone crucified is accursed," God's (crucified) Anointed provided freedom from the curse by becoming a curse on behalf of others. (Deut 21:23, quoted in Gal 3:13)
6. With that freedom, even non-Jews can share in Abraham's blessing through God's Anointed, Jesus, which means they receive the promise through his act of trust. (Gal 3:14)

The curse of Jesus' particular kind of death, "hanging on a tree" ("obedience to the point of death on a cross," Phil 2:8), amounted to "buying us back from such a curse," the way a slave is bought back from its master. Because this death exemplified total trust, it is an act of love for those who share in it (Gal 2:20) and thus participate in the blessing and promise to Abraham.

Paul relishes this "scandal of the cross" (Gal 5:11), making what appears to be accursed turn out to bring redemption. The conviction that "God raised Jesus from the dead" meant for Paul that the curse of the cross was turned into a blessing—a fulfillment of the promise to Abraham that through him all peoples would be blessed. The foundation was Abraham's trust, which counted as virtue.

What about the Law?

Paul's insights and arguments reflect his indebtedness to Scripture—using it in its Greek translation, yet his logical outcome seems to end up making the law unnecessary. Since the Mosaic law came 430 years after Abraham, it cannot annul the promise God made in the covenant with Abraham. That promise was based on total trust (Gal 3:17–18, 22), and if God is indeed trustworthy, then that promise is still valid. The law that came later did provide the discipline necessary to restrain sin, but it did so by putting everyone under the curse of the law. That condition was only changed when the curse was reversed by the faithful obedience of Jesus, God's Anointed. The law itself is not based on trust, and it cannot make anyone virtuous (Rom 8:3–4). It cannot count trust as virtue—the way God did for Abraham.

At the same time, trust does not invalidate the law (Rom 3:31). It's just that anyone who has already experienced vindication through total trust has no need to keep distinctive ethnic practices. On the other hand, those who adopt the traditional customs come under the threat of the law's curse and become obligated to adhere to all its prescriptions (Gal 5:2–6).

The law was effective, however, in calling attention to sin (Rom 3:20; Gal 3:19). Keeping the customs prescribed in the Mosaic tradition allows those in the covenant to maintain their status as members of the covenant. However, there is no basis in the law for claiming that God's promises would be available to other people if only they adopted these distinctive ethnic practices. Such favoritism would invalidate God's impartiality. Nothing less than God's own trustworthiness is at stake for Paul.

Paul's analysis of the human condition and his solution to the problem allow him to affirm his commitment to Jewish monotheism and to express it in universal terms. For Paul this is the best of both worlds.

Chapter Six

Paul: A New Perspective

John L. White

R eading several new works on Paul in recent years, it seems
at first they emphasize different things as the key to the
apostle's theology. On reflection, however, many of the works
point in the same direction, a direction counter to the prevailing
picture of Paul. Three of these problematic views, that the new
works call into question, comprise a background for identifying
the new way in which Paul is being understood. The composite
picture of Paul that emerges is my own work, though many of
the details derive from these recent interpreters.

The first view that calls for consideration is the way Paul's
idea of salvation has been interpreted in terms of modem values.
In his essay in 1960, "The Apostle Paul and the Introspective
Conscience of the West," Krister Stendahl claims that Rudolf
Bultmann, a noted biblical scholar, interpreted Paul in an overly
personal way. Worse yet, according to Stendahl, Bultmann is
typical of the Lutheran view of salvation, which dominates the
understanding of Paul in the West.

From Luther onward, Paul has been interpreted as provid-
ing a cure for the individual's guilty conscience. But before this,

The Fourth R 6,6 (1993), pp. 11–14

Stendahl says, up to the time of Augustine, Christianity did not interpret Paul in terms of *personal* liberation from the law. Rather, Christianity emphasized two *social* aspects: (1) the new relation to God in Christ replaces Moses' law as the basis of being God's people; and (2) because the Messiah has arrived, Gentiles may also become God's people without first becoming Jews. Thus, Paul's emphasis on "justification by faith" answered the social question of how Gentiles become God's people. But Paul did not intend to address the personal difficulties in obeying the law.

A second problem in the interpretation of Paul is the extent to which scholars may assume that Christianity was insulated from non-Jewish culture. To be sure, Christianity did arise out of Judaism. But Jews were subject to the same cultural forces that were influencing paganism. Everyone was breathing the same cultural air. Even Moses' law was being defined more universally and in a less racially specific way in Paul's day.

Nonetheless, many interpreters suggest Christianity was virtually uncontaminated by its culture. One bizarre expression of this view of insulation is found in Martin Hengel's 1993 presidential address at the Society of New Testament Studies. Although Hengel acknowledged that no oriental religion integrated so much of Hellenistic civilization as Judaism did, he still argued that Christianity was somehow virtually untouched by pagan influence. Although the church arose out of Judaism, a religion that *was* influenced by the prevailing culture, Christianity was strangely *not* influenced by it! Like the mythical Athena, it seems Christianity was born fully mature, direct from the head of God.

It is precisely the above double-talk that Jonathan Z. Smith criticizes in his book *Drudgery Divine*. Smith says there is a Protestant myth which assumes the earliest stage of Christianity ("Apostolic" Christianity) was untouched by its contemporary culture. It was only corrupted in "post-apostolic" times by mixing with paganism. This view proceeds to equate the "magical idea" of the Catholic Mass with Christian degeneration into the superstitious practices of the pagan mysteries. By contrast, the same viewpoint engenders the belief that Protestantism represents a restoration of Christianity's "pristine" origins.

This idea of pristine Christianity is untenable. It can hardly be doubted, at least for Paul, that the picture of baptismal immersion as "dying with Christ" parallels ritualistic practices in the mystery religions. Nor can we deny the mysteries' influence on Paul's picture of resurrection as the *"putting on* of Christ." Despite the modernizing emphasis attributed to Bultmann above, he *has* acknowledged the influence of the mystery cults on Paul. Moreover, in commenting on Paul's depiction of baptism as mystical participation in Christ's death, Bultmann states that something *objective* happens. The sacrament is not merely a symbol of the convert's subjective process.

Although Stendahl rightly criticizes Bultmann for interpreting Paul in modern existential terms, Stendahl grants Paul far less cultural elasticity than Bultmann does. For Stendahl assumes that even after Paul turned from being a persecutor to an advocate of the church, he continued to have a legalistic mindset. By insisting on the Gentiles' legal *release* from Moses' law, Stendahl assumes Paul never escaped from his earlier Pharisaic idea of God as lawgiver and judge. Stendahl admits that *"justification* by faith" is emphasized only in Romans and Galatians, but he makes it nonetheless the key to Paul's idea of Jewish-Gentile relations. Worse, he argues that, because of excessive concern with the principle of liberation from Moses' law, Paul's ministry was divisive and ineffective.

The third view of Paul that calls for reconsideration is overemphasis on the importance of his culture for determining the content of his letters. There is over-emphasis on the importance of sociological factors for understanding Paul's letters. And there is an over-emphasis on the external circumstances which led Paul to write letters. As for the letters, several interpreters assume that throughout his ministry, Paul had to deal with one problem—he had to defend himself against a "judaizing" movement that continuously hounded him. Others say that there is no continuity from one letter to another, because Paul had to deal with different issues on each occasion. In either case, it is assumed the content of his letters was occasioned by external issues and not factors inherent to Paul himself.

In contrast, certain scholars now argue that Paul himself is the source of the theological similarities in his letters. Thus, Daniel Patte states in his book *Paul's Faith and the Power of the Gospel* that Paul himself is the source of the recurring convictions that

pervade his letters. Although Paul's convictional logic does not
exhibit itself in simple, linear argumentation, Patte says the pattern is evident in Paul's distinctive use of emotional language, in
is graphic images, and in his repetition of key themes.

Similarly, Norman Petersen argues in his book *Rediscovering
Paul* that Paul's own symbolic world view is the organizing
principle behind the letters. In particular, Petersen illustrates the
influence of "fictional" reality on the way Paul composed his letter to Philemon. The literal circumstance is that Philemon's slave
Onesimus had run away and Paul found it necessary to intervene
on behalf of Onesimus. However, in the letter itself, fictional
relationships take priority over the actual master-slave relationship. Why? Because for Paul, the relation between Philemon and
Onesimus as spiritual "brothers" must takes precedence over the
master-slave relationship of Philemon's actual household.

The above example also suggests that sociological analysis of
Paul's culture is not adequate by itself to understand Paul. Paul
manipulates social categories to serve his own purposes. So we
must attend to the ways he departs from conventions and to his
reasons for doing so.

Three problematic elements in the interpretation of Paul are
identified; interpreters who provide alternative views are named.
Now we can compose a new picture.

Beginning with emphases found in Petersen and Patte, it is
clear Paul had little trouble engaging Gentiles in an appealing and
concrete way. Our earlier comments about Paul's use of imagery
from the mysteries indicate the same thing. "Justification by faith"
is not only too Jewish to be the key to Paul's theology, it is too
abstract. To be sure, Paul uses this formulation in Romans and
Galatians, where Jewish issues are at the fore, but even in these
letters the root image of God is not that of lawgiver.

The importance of metaphor to Paul, along with his adapta-
tion of social conventions in the service of his symbolic world
view, suggest he thought about God's salvation in Christ in an
analogical way. Paul was not fixed rigidly on the Jewishness of
that salvation, at least not on its racial and historical specificity. In
fact, Paul was not fixated on Christ.

To Paul, Christ was obviously important as the mediator of
God's salvation. But Paul was not concerned with what was

unique or unrepeatable about Christ's death and resurrection. Rather, the events illustrate what is "typical" of God's power as creator. In the resurrection, God proves himself able, in an especially personal way, to create life out of death. Paul persuaded Gentiles to share Christ's trust in God's creative power over destructive circumstances and, thereby, to become recipients of the same power. This was no theoretical hope in resurrection from an eventual literal death. New life was a present reality, already lifting converts above forces analogous to those that attacked Jesus and over which he was victorious. The reality of the new life was experienced socially in fellowship with others, not in isolation from the community. So far as Paul's own Jewish sensibilities were concerned, he found an analogy for God's life-giving power in Abraham. Abraham became the father of God's people not because he himself had done anything to deserve the status but by means of God's power to create life out of Abraham and Sarah's barrenness.

In short, because of Paul's experience of the resurrected Christ, his monotheism took on a new character—God as creator. It was no longer the idea of lawgiver and judge that held the key to God's identity. It is his character as creator. The same God who created the universe is now liberating it and recreating it according to the pattern exhibited in Christ and Abraham.

In light of Paul's emphasis on God's generative power, it is hardly accidental that he refers to the church at Corinth as God's fertile field, nor that he often uses agricultural images of fertility. The explosive power of nature's growth out of apparent death corresponds to the power of Christ's resurrection. Agricultural images resonated with Gentile devotees of the mystery cults who participated in nature's power over sterile forces.

Although nature's liveliness embodied something essential about the divine power, it was finally neither personal enough nor social enough to capture God's complete character. Even more important than the agricultural metaphors, consequently, was Paul's image of the family as a symbol of the church. Above all, God is the "father," who procreates the family's offspring. Because of his spiritual generation from death, Christ is both "first-born" son from the dead and the mature son whose trust in God made him a worthy heir. In his maturity, he is the spiritual household's "lord." In turn, converts who participate in the generative power exhibited in Christ are God's "sons" and "daughters." In their relation to each other, they are spiritual siblings, "brethren."

In conclusion, Paul's most essential idea of God is his beneficial, generative power. Due to the abstract and impersonal nature of the idea of creator, Paul personalized God's creativity by identifying it as a father's procreative and nurturing power. Indeed, Paul refers explicitly to God's fatherly affection. This corresponds to the personal way Jesus addressed God as *abba* ("daddy"). Consequently, Paul weds the cosmic principle of God's generative power as creator to God's personal, procreative power as father. This combination of universal and particular corresponds to the Jewish idea of election. But Paul's image of God as creator has the advantage of being especially suggestive of the idea that the church's present relation with God as "father" will become the universal experience of all creation:

> Creation itself will be set free from its bondage to decay
> and obtain the glorious liberty of the children of God.
> (Rom 8:21)

Works Consulted

Baur, F. C. *Paul, His Life and Works*. 2 vols. London: Williams and Norgate, 1875–1876.

Beker, J. Christiaan. *The Triumph of God*. Minneapolis: Fortress, 1990.

Boyarin, Daniel. *A Radical Jew. Paul and the Politics of Identity*. Berkeley: University of California Press, 1994.

Bultmann, Rudolf. *Theology of the New Testament*. 2 vols. New York: Scribners, 1952 and 1955.

Davies, W. D. *Paul and Rabbinic Judaism*. New York: Harper and Row, 1948.

Deissmann, Adolf. *St. Paul: A Study in Social and Religious History*. New York: Doran, 1926.

Dewey, Arthur, Roy W. Hoover, Lane C. McGaughy, and Daryl C Schmidt. *The Authentic Letters of Paul*. Salem, OR: Polebridge, 2010.

Dunn, James D. G. *The Theology of Paul the Apostle*. Edinburgh, 1998.

Funk, Robert. *Honest to Jesus*. San Francisco: HarperCollins, 1996.

Harnack, Adolf. *What Is Christianity?* (Reprint of 1900 translation). New York: Harper and Row, 1957.

Hurd, John. *The Origins of 1 Corinthians*. New York: Seabury, 1965.

Jenks, Gregory C. "What Paul Knew About Jesus." *The Fourth R* 12,1 (January–February 1999), pp. 3–12.

Knox, John. *Chapters in a Life of Paul*. Nashville: Abingdon, 1950. Revision 1987.

Lüdemann, Gerd. *Paul, Apostle to the Gentiles*. Philadelphia: Fortress, 1984.

Miller, Robert J., ed. *The Complete Gospels*. Sonoma, CA: Polebridge Press, 2010.

Moo, Douglas J. "The Theology of Romans 9–11. A Response to E. Elizabeth Johnson." In David M. Hay & E. Elizabeth Johnson (eds.), *Pauline Theology*, Vol. 3: *Romans*. Minneapolis: Fortress, 1995, 240–58.

Patte, Daniel. *Paul's Faith and the Power of the Gospel*. Philadelphia: Fortress, 1983.

Patterson, Stephen, John Kloppenborg, Marvin Meyer, and Michael Steinhauser. *Q Thomas Reader*. Sonoma: Polebridge, 1990.

Pervo, Richard I. *Dating Acts. Between the Evangelists and the Apologists*. Santa Rosa, CA: Polebridge, 2006.

Petersen, Norman. *Rediscovering Paul*. Philadelphia: Fortress, 1985.

Sanders, E. P. *Paul and Palestinian Judaism*. Philadelphia: Fortress, 1977.

_____. *Paul, the Law and the Jewish People*. Philadelphia: Fortress, 1983.

_____. *Paul*. Philadelphia: Fortress, 1981.

Sandmel, Samuel. *A Jewish Understanding of the New Testament*. Cincinnati: Hebrew Union College Press, 1977.

_____. *The Genius of Paul*. New York: Farrar, Straus & Cudahy, 1979.

Schweitzer, Albert. *Paul and His Interpreters*. New York: Macmillan, 1912.

_____. *The Mysticism of Paul the Apostle*. London, 1930. Reprint 1998.

_____. *The Quest of the Historical Jesus*. New York: H. Holt and Co.

Segal, Alan F. *Paul the Convert: The Apostolate and the Apostasy of Saul the Pharisee*. New Haven: Yale University, 1990.

White, John. *The Apostle of God. Paul and the Promise of Abraham*. Peabody, MA: Hendrickson, 1999.

Witherington III, Ben. *The Paul Quest: The Renewed Search for the Jew of Tarsus*. Downers Grove: Intervarsity Press, 1998.

Discussion Questions

Chapter 1

Gerd Lüdemann, *"Paul—an Obituary"*

1. Before you begin reading Lüdemann's essay, draw up a short description of who you think Paul was and what he was about.
2. Why is Paul a major influence on Christianity?
3. Why does Paul have such a problem with a suffering Messiah? Why is this the critical problem for Pau? How does Lüdemann see Paul solving this problem?
4. The cosmic drama of redemption envisions as pivotal the salvation of the Gentiles. How does Lüdemann see this playing out?
5. What precisely is the conflict Lüdemann refers to? What is its cause?
6. How was the unity of the church maintained and at what price? How does the collection for Jerusalem figure into this solution?
7. How does Romans 9-11 take back everything Paul has written earlier in the letter? Where is the contradiction to which Lüdemann is pointing?
8. What is the explicit charge of Paul's opponents? How does Lüdemann evaluate the legitimacy of this charge?
9. What constitutes the conflict between Paul and Greek thought as exemplified by his speech at Athens?
10. How much of Lüdemann's picture of Paul is drawn from Acts? What happens to the picture of Paul if Acts is removed?

Chapter 2
Heikki Räisänen, *"A Controversial Jew"*

1. Räisänen states, "The emergence of Christianity as a new religion, distinct from Judaism, was a long process, a chain reaction in which one thing led to another." What do you think those stages might be? Can you sketch out such an emergence? When do you think Christianity clearly becomes separate from Judaism?

2. What does Räisänen think is Paul's problem with those who believe Jesus is the Messiah? What is his bold new interpretation of Judaism?

3. How does Paul resemble Philo?

4. Who are these "conservative Jesus-believers"? What are their characteristics?

5. How does Paul differ from the Hellenists? What is his radical understanding of the Torah?

6. 1 Cor. 9:19–22 is a linchpin in Räisänen's argument. What does he see Paul doing in this saying? Does he see Paul being duplicitous?

7. What does it tell you about Paul that he was punished by the synagogue with whippings (2 Cor 11:24)?

8. What are the steps in Paul's argument that allows the church to replace the people of Israel?

9. Can you explain what Räisänen sees as the contradiction between Galatians and Romans? What role does the context of these two letters play in Paul's argument?

10. What is Räisänen's argument that Paul views God in Romans 9 as a tyrant? How does he see Paul redefining Israel so as not to include ethnic Israel?

11. In Romans 11 is Paul changing course? How does this argument relate to the apparent rejection of ethnic Israel in Romans 9? Why does Paul abandon the predestination argument?

Chapter 3
James Veitch, *"Spotlight on St. Paul"*

1. Räisänen suspects those who demand an inner consistency in Paul of falling back on the doctrine of inspiration and using Paul as an authority. Veitch likewise warns against understand-

ing Paul as authority. What are both of these author's concerned about? What is the risk? How should we view Paul?

2. Why and how does an historical investigation of Jesus or Paul threaten the church?

3. In Baur's effort to shift the understanding of Paul from theology to history, he situated Paul within the debate between Jewish and Hellenistic Christians. What is the significance of this shift and how does it play out?

4. Why is it inappropriate (or appropriate depending upon your point of view) to resolve historical issues in the study of Paul by means of theology? Give an example of this problem.

5. Why does Veitch think Schweitzer's apocalyptic Jesus became acceptable to the church in the twentieth century?

6. What is common between Jesus and Paul in Schweitzer's view and why was this important according to Veitch in the acceptance of Schweitzer's view?

7. How does Bultmann reinterpret Paul's apocalyptic message as an existential message?

8. What is radical about Davies insistence that Paul was and remained a Jew?

9. Why does Veitch see Paul at the center of the church's search for identity?

10. What does it mean to say that Paul was a cultural critic of Judaism? Does that put him within or outside of Judaism?

Chapter 4
John White, *"The Second Founder of Christianity"*

1. White sees Paul as a convert to Hellenistic Jewish Christianity. How was this movement Jewish and what was Paul's objection to it before his conversion?

2. What two traditions does White see emerging from Paul? How did the two traditions interpret Paul differently? What are the practical outcomes of such different interpretations? In your judgment which one is the correct interpretation of Paul?

3. How does White see Paul's view of God as parallel or similar to that of Jesus? How does White see Paul's view of God as functioning like Jesus' parables? What do you make of the claim?

4. Why does Paul place a strong emphasis on the uncleanness and lawlessness of Jesus' death? Why was Jesus' death nonsense within the terms of the Jewish law?

5. Why is Abraham a good model for the potential Gentile convert to both Judaism and Christianity?

6. According to White what role does adoption play in Paul's understanding of Gentile conversion?

7. How is Jesus' death and resurrection like the conception and birth of Abraham' son Isaac?

8. How do James, Peter and Paul represent three different types of Christianity? What does this tell you about unity and diversity in early Christianity?

9. Why does White reject picture of Paul in Acts' always going first to the synagogue? Why does White argue that Paul's Gentile converts for the most part did not have previous contact with the synagogue? How do you evaluate his argument?

10. What was Paul's paradoxical view of God? Why was it a paradox? Why did Paul adopt this view of God?

11. How do Paul's four metaphors for the church in 1 Corinthians derive from his paradoxical view of God?

Chapter 5
Daryl Schmidt, *"Making Sense of Paul."*

1. For Schmidt what problem is Paul trying to solve? Why is this problem central for Paul?

2. What are Paul's two basic assumptions? Where does he derive these assumptions?

3. What is Paul's summary of the human condition? From where does he derive this summary? How is this the universal problem?

4. What is the universal solution to the universal problem?

5. In the story of Abraham what are the three steps that Paul employs to solve his problem?

6. Why does trust in God's accounting system count against sin?

7. How is Abraham's total trust like Jesus' total trust? What is God's response in each case? What ties Abraham and Jesus together for Paul?

8. How is the death of Jesus part of God's scheme?
9. How is the curse of the cross turned into a blessing?
10. What was the purpose of the Mosaic law?

Chapter 6
John White, *"Paul: A New Perspective"*

1. What is the source of interpreting Paul as answering the problem of personal guilt? Does Paul really address this problem?
2. What three factors in some recent scholarship does White see as problematic? Why are they problematic?
3. Why does White reject justification by faith as the key to Paul?
4. What is the significance of Paul's thought as analogical? How does this relate to Jesus' uniqueness? What does Paul see as the basic pattern of God's activity?
5. Why is the family the basic pattern (analogy) for Paul?
6. How does Paul elaborate or play out the family metaphor?